Drawing insight

Communicating Development Through Animation

With a Foreword by

Roy Disney

Edited by

Joyce Greene & Deborah Reber

Original Book Illustrations by

Christian Clark

Southbound

Penang

Published in Malaysia by
Southbound Sdn. Bhd.
9 College Square
10250 Penang
Malaysia
Fax: 60-4-228 1758
Internet: chin@south.pc.my

ISBN 983-9054-14-7

Printed by Phoenix Press
Penang, Malaysia

Typeset by Typographics
in 10.5/13 pt. Palatino

*The Publishers gratefully acknowledge
the assistance of the following members of the
animation and development communities in the
publication of this book:*

*Radio, Television & Film Section at UNICEF New York
Special thanks to Walt Disney Feature Animation
Morten Giersing
William Hetzer
Mehr Khan
Editorial Assistant:
Shantha Bloemen*

Perpustakaan Negara Malaysia
Cataloguing-in-Publication Data

Drawing insight: communicating development through animation /
with a foreword by Roy Disney.
ISBN 983-9054-14-7
1. Animation (Cinematography). 2. Animated films.
I. Disney, Roy
791.433

Contents

Dedication

This book is dedicated to

JAMES P. GRANT

the late Executive Director of UNICEF
who devoted himself to improving the lives
of children everywhere.

Jim Grant was keenly aware of animation's power to reach children and their parents with vital information they need to survive and develop. He was instrumental in convening the first Animation For Development Workshop in Prague in 1990, and cared deeply about UNICEF's work with the animation industry until his death in January 1995.

James P. Grant, the late Executive Director of UNICEF, with a child in Cote d'Ivoire

Foreword

Roy Disney

© The Walt Disney Company

You might think that recent Disney films such as *The Lion King* and UNICEF's early animated health messages are at the farthest extremes of the animation art form. In a technical sense, you'd be right.

But, in a very real way, the Disney and UNICEF films have a great deal in common.

They both had to overcome major hurdles in order to get made — and they both prove what a uniquely effective medium animation is.

In the case of the Disney films, it wasn't very many years ago that everyone believed animated films were way too expensive, and that they were just for kids. A lot of people thought it was foolhardy for us to pour millions of dollars into new animation technology. As our recent films have proved, we couldn't have spent our money more wisely. Not only have these films done spectacularly well at the box office . . . but, because of the timeless appeal of animation, they can be counted on to continue to enchant audiences for generations to come.

In much the same way, the UNICEF animated films had to overcome the idea that animation was too expensive a medium for a development organisation — the idea that it would be faster and cheaper to simply videotape an announcer speaking about the importance of immunisation, rather than to create an animated film from scratch on the subject.

Fortunately, these concerns were overcome. In terms of effectiveness, the UNICEF animated films that resulted are a bargain. Just like the Disney films, they immediately grab the attention of viewers, especially young ones. And, like the Disney films, they will be as fresh and effective 50 years from now as they are today. In fact, I would venture to say that these films will only become dated once the problems they address are solved.

Of course, I'm a bit biased when it comes to the subject of animation. My uncle created some of the greatest animated films of all time, and my father was instrumental in getting these films made. Walt was always aware of the power of animation. He knew that it was an extraordinary medium for teaching. In fact, Walt always used to say that he thought of himself as an educator who entertained. He thought animation was one of the best tools an educator ever had. As he put it: "Give 'em an ounce of treatment . . . and a ton of treat."

I have inherited both my uncle's and my father's love of animation. That's why I was so excited when the opportunity arose for The Walt Disney Company to work with UNICEF to train animators from developing countries. We could be like most corporations and just give money. But I like to think we're giving something more valuable. Instead of giving a fund of dollars, we're giving a fund of knowledge and experience. The fact is, at Disney, our greatest asset isn't our balance sheet. It's our heritage. And this is what we're trying to share.

Our involvement with UNICEF began during Mickey Mouse's 60th birthday at the United Nations. That's when we first met the late Executive Director of UNICEF, Jim Grant, and the idea emerged that our company might have something unique to offer UNICEF.

Then came the first Animation for Development Workshop in Prague, when Max Howard, former Senior Vice President of Administration for Walt Disney Feature Animation, got involved in a big way. The Prague conference began Disney's work with UNICEF. But it was the animation workshop in Jamaica that truly made believers of us.

Animation is a painstaking process. It takes many years to fully train an animator, and it generally takes four years to produce a single animated feature film. So it was with some hesitation that we set up the Jamaica Workshop, which brought 17 artists from 12 countries together to try to teach them how to make an animated film in just two weeks. Four people from our Disney animation staff helped with the training programme and, to everyone's amazement, the artists managed to produce a complete — and very effective — film at the end of the course. The film, *Johnny Sad Boy*, has unmistakable power and impact as it deals in a mere 50 seconds with the terribly difficult and terribly important issue of child abuse.

Indeed, this is the real strength of animation. It can tackle any subject. It can take us into the single cell of an amoeba or out into outer space. It can give us talking mice or wooden boys, flying dragons or singing mermaids. It can show us the wonder of the earth's creation, or the potential that lies in each and every one of us. Animation can not only portray anything, but can do so in such a way as to grab the attention of anyone of any age, of any culture here on earth.

This ability of animation to universally communicate even the most abstract of concepts is what makes it such an invaluable tool. It's all well and good to use animation to tell classic fairy tales, but UNICEF's mission is truly of a higher magnitude. It's about saving and enriching the lives of young people around the word. To do this, it must relate health, nutrition and lifestyle concepts that are often complicated and remote. Animation can make them real and immediate.

When we talk about abstract — but critically important — subjects, I can think of none greater than teenage pregnancy. In rich and poor nations alike, children are having children. If we could solve this one single problem, we would be making a major assault against the cycle of poverty. The magnitude of the problem is huge, and it is a tremendously difficult issue to communicate to teenagers who aren't always concerned about the consequences of their actions. Guy O'Neal, an intern at our animation studio at Walt Disney World, produced a short film on this issue during his internship. He combined his personal talent with the communication possibilities of animation to give us a strong message on this difficult issue.

Our internship programme was established to train talented young American artists in animation. However, we are now reserving one of the slots to train an artist from a developing country during each internship cycle, so that he or she can then go back home to create animation for UNICEF. As well as the internship and the Jamaica Workshop, a number of our artists have travelled to Ecuador to help Cinearte, a local animation company, with the creation of UNICEF's Maximo character.

I want to stress that in no way are we trying to teach people that Disney's way of doing animation is the only way. Not only would this be wrong — it would be foolish. Since animation is truly an unlimited art form, there is no right or wrong way to do it. Among the American studios, Disney definitely has a certain style. So do Warner Brothers and Hanna-Barbera and the people at Fox who produce *The Simpsons*. They're all effective and successful. It is our hope that the budding animators we are helping to train will find their own style which will not just be as good as ours, but will truly be better because it will be infused with an understanding of the people and culture they are trying to reach.

What's more, the fact is that we learn at least as much from our students as they do from us. Traditionally, the animator's life is pretty much an ivory tower existence. Day after day, they sit at their desks creating hundreds of drawings, without much contact with anyone except other animators. Our involvement with UNICEF has allowed our artists to break out of this shell and, bonded by a love of animation, embark on a joint journey of discovery with artists from around the world. We hope that those who have joined us on this journey have benefited from the exchange. We know we have.

You'll read later in this book about our work with UNICEF on the Maximo project. The first film in this series, dealing with immunisation, took Cinearte a year to produce. The second, on iodised salt, took four months. This is the ultimate achievement of UNICEF's animation initiative. Not only is the world benefiting from some outstanding and creative public health messages, but the talented creators of those messages are on the road to productive self-sufficiency.

I've always been a big believer in the maxim that if you give a person a fish, he'll eat for a day; but if you teach a person to fish, he'll eat for the rest of his life. That's what I like to think we're doing through our involvement with UNICEF. The artists who are creating these films for UNICEF are now embarking on careers of their own. They, in turn, will be teaching others the art of animation. And so, in a small way, we're taking another whack at the cycle of poverty and dependence.

After all, the ultimate goal of Disney's work with UNICEF is to put itself out of business by creating a world where children are healthy and their parents are leading productive and fulfilling lives. At Disney, we feel privileged to be able to make a contribution towards bringing that day a little closer.

Editors' Preface

About UNICEF

The United Nations Children's Fund is, as its name implies, the UN agency that deals with children. We celebrate our 50th anniversary in 1996, which means we are a year younger than the United Nations itself. Although the governments of the world are our boss, our job is to tell them — and to tell the public at large — that they can and must do far better by the world's children, and then to help them do so.

© UNICEF, Pirozzi

A young girl carrying food in Nigeria

What we are trying to do in the 140 developing countries where we have programmes of cooperation is to harness the extraordinary technological and scientific capacity of this age to benefit not just a privileged minority of children, but all children, especially the children of the more than one billion poor around the world living on about a dollar a day.

We believe that by saving children's lives —some 25 million since the mid-1980s — and by giving them a decent start in life, we can give each child a fighting chance against poverty. These children can then contribute to building more prosperous economies and more democratic societies, which in turn helps to slow population growth, eases stress on the environment, improves women's status and prevents wars.

UNICEF's constituency, the world's children, is the animation industry's primary audience, and all of us have a stake in their survival, protection and development.

UNICEF and Animation

UNICEF first used animation for advocacy purposes in the 1960s. But it wasn't until we used animation at community viewing centres in Nepal in the mid-1980s that we discovered how well the medium got vital information across to literate and non-literate audiences. In Nepal, animated features and shorts on health topics were often projected at night on to a white cloth suspended from a tree with the use of a generator. A Nepalese presenter would mimic the voices of the characters over the megaphone.

© UNICEF, L. Goldsmith

We have come a long way since then, thanks to our partnership with leading pioneers and key players in the field of animation. Today, UNICEF is involved in major animation projects that will be outlined in detail later in this book. Thanks to partners like Disney, Hanna-Barbera, ASIFA, Children's Television Workshop and Televisa, we are getting our messages across in innovative, more effective ways to ever-larger audiences.

Animation for Development

There have been a number of major developments for children in recent years.

The 1990 World Summit for Children and the almost universal ratification of the Convention on the Rights of the Child have proved that—with the commitment of governments and peoples—tremendous strides for children can be made. How does animation fit in to the process of achieving these goals? I truly believe that animation can do much more than "fit in" to this process. It can help make it happen.

Most of the goals for children can only be reached if there is strong public mobilisation

Children at school in Mauritania

and social commitment. What we have done with animation since those early days in Nepal has proved that this mobilisation and commitment can be achieved—and that an integrated communications strategy, including animation, is a key part of the process.

How Animation Can Make A Difference

We believe that animation can be an important catalyst — a global communications medium that can help make the world a better place for our children. There are many areas where UNICEF feels animation can make a difference.

The communications revolution has given us the capacity to reach the world's developing nations and poor populations, even as social and economic exclusion continues to be the chief characteristic of most national and global economic systems. This imposes an ethical responsibility on communicators—to use the tools of the communication revolution, including animation, to help relieve suffering and alleviate poverty. It also provides a business opportunity — to invest in the future prosperity of poor countries and communities that are providing new audiences and new markets for animation industry products.

The animation industry must avoid the temptation to write off the developing countries. The so-called Asian Tigers were dismissed by many economists as hopeless twenty years ago, yet today they produce and consume much of the world's industrial output. There is much to be gained—financially, socially and ethically—from focusing more of our energies and creativity on developing countries, as well as on poor communities in the richer nations.

Each generation needs new heroes and role models. Through television, movies, video games and interactive media, animation increasingly defines the heroes and villains that are our children's paradigms of good and evil and right and wrong. Young peoples' values and attitudes are heavily influenced by the mass media. If the "good guys" on television and in the movies are violent, hate-filled and intolerant of "bad guys" whose "badness" consists of little more than being different from them, we have a formula for perpetuating ethnic, racial and religious strife. If girls and boys are portrayed in a traditional, stereotyped way, there is little hope of attaining gender equality, empowerment of women and resilient families.

On the other hand, we know that solid values and appropriate role models can make for good, money-making entertainment. The animation industry has done a vast amount of research on how television, movies and video games influence young viewers. At the same time, UNICEF has a vast amount of information on how to protect young people's health and promote their development. Can we not marry these two categories of knowledge, providing our children with appropriate role models and strong values?

There is so much more that can be done to solve very urgent problems we are facing. An example of how animation can help was *Break the Silence - Kids Against Child Abuse*, a documentary that, through animated images created by John Canemaker, explained the sensitive issue of child abuse and offered solutions. In Mexico, deaths from diarrhoeal dehydration have been halved in three years, thanks in part to a remarkably effective campaign using animated spots on television. Animation is helping countries all over the world to achieve the goals set at the World Summit for Children. But far more can be done.

We at UNICEF believe the animation industry stands to gain from building the animation capacity of developing countries. We all know that the vast markets of the developing world will never be fully served by imports. The productions of culturally-sensitive, locally-relevant animated features and shorts, supported by major animation studios in industrialised countries, could tap this extraordinary potential. We believe that there is a tremendous repository of talent, new ideas and creative approaches in the developing world that can enrich animation.

Another way animation can help is just by making children smile. Children caught up in the horror of war need relief from images of terror and death, and need ways to get through their feelings of grief and anger. We are coming to better understand the complex psycho-social mechanism of war trauma among children and are searching for appropriate interventions that can be applied to groups as well as individuals. We believe that cartoons should be part of our response. Surely we can stock our relief supplies with scores of cartoons and animated shorts that can help children heal and laugh again.

There are many more ways in which animation can make a difference. We hope that commercial partnerships can be formed in which we bring entertainment together, and that in the future UNICEF will be able to generate funds through merchandising as a result of these successful partnerships.

A Challenge to the Industry

These are some of the ways we are seeking the animation industry's assistance in achieving drastic, measurable progress for children in the rest of this decade and into the next century. We at UNICEF want to challenge the industry to work with us—to develop new ways to reach into as many corners of the world as we can with as many messages as we can.

The *American Heritage Dictionary* defines animation first and foremost as "the act, process or result of imparting life, interest, spirit, motion, or activity." It is because animation imparts life, interest, spirit, motion and activity that we believe the industry truly has the power to make tremendous progress for children in the years to come.

Introduction

William Hetzer

UNICEF and Children

UNICEF was created by the United Nations General Assembly in 1946 to meet the emergency needs of children in the aftermath of World War II in Europe. Today, it is striving to meet the long term needs of children living in poverty in developing countries. UNICEF is the only United Nations organisation dedicated exclusively to children and it works on behalf of children on the basis of need, without discrimination with regard to race, creed, nationality, status or political belief.

Nearly 13 million children in the developing world die each year from largely preventable causes. UNICEF recognises the tremendous power of mass communications to spread messages that can help save those lives. UNICEF is helping countries to keep their promises to improve the lives of children by cooperating on detailed national programmes of action for children.

Immunisation: Today, children can be protected from a number of life-threatening diseases such as measles, tuberculosis, tetanus, diphtheria, whooping cough and polio. In 1990, universal child immunisation was achieved, meaning 8 out of every 10 children was immunised, saving 3 million young lives every year.

Oral Rehydration Therapy (ORT): ORT is a simple solution of water, salt and sugar that saves the lives of children suffering from dehydration by diarrhoea. Today, 3 million children still die every year from diarrhoea.

Salt Iodisation: Iodine deficiency is the single greatest cause of preventable mental retardation in the world and is easily solved by iodising salt. 120,000 children every year are born mentally and physically impaired because their mothers didn't get enough iodine in their diets.

Safe Water & Sanitation: In the developing world, over 4 million young children die every year from diseases associated with unsafe water. UNICEF helps provide sanitation facilities to the nearly 1.9 billion people around world who lack them.

Safe Motherhood: Every year 500,000 women and teens die and millions of others suffer disabling and lifelong injuries from causes related to pregnancy and childbirth.

Vitamin A: Every year, 250,000 children in the developing world are permanently blinded and millions more suffer night blindness due to vitamin A deficiency. It is a factor in 20-30% of child deaths in developing countries every year.

Breastfeeding: It is especially valuable for infants to be fed nothing but breastmilk for the first six months of life — the period when they are least resistant to infections and most need the nurture and nutrition breastfeeding alone confers. The baby-friendly hospital initiative encourages breastfeeding in hospitals and at home.

Education for All: A quarter of the world's population is illiterate and millions of children, more girls than boys, never go to school. UNICEF works with UNESCO to train teachers and make primary education free and compulsory for every child.

Children in Especially Difficult Circumstances: As many as 200 million children in the world work for their own and/or their families' survival. They labour in oppressive and dangerous factory jobs, in domestic service, on the streets of cities and towns or in degrading conditions of sexual exploitation.

Girls: Girls face discrimination that often threatens their lives and well-being from the moment of birth throughout their life span. Girls receive less food and medical care than boys and far less education, and are condemned to lives of poor health, diminished expectations and reduced capacity.

AIDS: AIDS is a public health crisis around the world and is undoing many of the gains achieved in children's health over the past decade. 1 million children are believed to be infected with HIV and this is increasing at an alarming rate. By the year 2000, nearly 10 million children will have been orphaned by AIDS.

Emergencies: UNICEF meets the needs of children and women affected by wars, civil strife and natural calamities, supplying food, medicine and clean water as emergencies arise. During the past decade, war and civil strife have left an estimated 1 million children orphaned or separated from their parents, 12 million homeless and some 10 million affected by psychological trauma.

Convention on the Rights of the Child: In 1990, the United Nations signed the Convention on the Rights of the Child, a UN Charter which sets out a unique spectrum of rights for children, specifying social and economic as well as civil and political rights for the first time in one instrument. The Convention recognises the rights of all children to develop physically, mentally and socially to their fullest potential, to express their opinions freely, and to participate in decisions affecting their future. As of May 1995, the Convention has been ratified by 174 countries. The Convention has become the driving force behind UNICEF's actions for children, and with the support of the creative media, strategies can be implemented that will reinforce the rights outlined in the Convention and ensure better and healthier lives for all children.

Meena is UNICEF's animated series on the South Asian girl child

UNICEF and Animation

A key part of UNICEF's role in implementing these programmes to increase development and behavioural change is raising the world's awareness and mobilising its resources in favour of children. From the start, UNICEF has always used radio, film and video productions, soap operas and street theatre, leaflets, posters and public meetings to help spread new information about children's health, welfare and rights. However, in the past several years, UNICEF has begun to utilise a new medium of communication to convey these important messages — with great results. That medium is animation.

UNICEF's mandate to communicate is urgent — the quality of a child's life may depend on it. The full dimension of how animation can be used within the UNICEF context to communicate life-saving messages is still unclear. What is apparent is that today, animation is hot.

Creativity within the medium is legendary. Any theme is possible for development, serious as well as light entertainment. Animation dominates the business pages of the trade press. Feature films like *The Lion King* are making record amounts of money. Spinoffs from famous animated stories have a life of their own. Characters appear on designer clothing, their images memorialised on t-shirts. Books, toys, games, CDs and videos sell like hot cakes. The Cartoon Network beams out on satellite — now viewed well beyond its original North American confines.

Animation is hot because it fascinates people and is highly entertaining. It has the ability to be quick and to the point, synthesising story and action to its elemental state. The absence of detail enhances understanding. Animation is cross cultural in outlook and has the ability to bridge the generation gap as well. Young and old enjoy a good story, especially when presented in a uniquely visual way. Lack of detail in geographic location, background setting and dress provide universal appeal. A less cluttered image emphasises plot and storyline.

Animation is hot because it's a medium that's young at heart. Story development can emphasise humour, outrageous behaviour, action, juxtaposition, inhibition — whatever the imagination can create. Animation can communicate any idea, contemporary or traditional, in inventive formats and with fresh insight.

© Kibushi NdjateWooto, Studio Malembe Malembe 1991

Preparation of the animated film *Le Crapaud chez ses beaux-parents* at Studio Malembe Malembe in Kinshasa, Zaire.

UNICEF's first active involvement in the world of animation came in 1990, when it hosted an Animation for Development Workshop in Prague. Representatives from UNICEF country offices met with animators from around the world to exchange ideas and experience, and consider the role that animation could play in conveying life-saving messages. The workshop was successful not only in convincing both UNICEF staff and industry leaders that animated film for development was a good idea, but it also started the ball rolling on several UNICEF animation initiatives such as the *Meena* and *Maximo* cartoons. A detailed description of the Prague workshop, as well as these animation initiatives, follows in this book.

In the years since the Prague workshop, it has become increasingly clear that UNICEF's work with animation can go far beyond our initial intent to communicate life-saving health information in an entertaining way. The success of the Meena initiative has shown that animation can be a catalyst for behaviour change. This could be key as we approach the more daunting health challenges of AIDS and health problems related to substance abuse.

As UNICEF moves forward in effectively utilising animation as a tool for development and change, organisational questions abound. How can UNICEF manage a complex animation project in terms of professional design, writing and production support, including financial planning and broadcast implementation? How can country offices best develop a project that is content perfect, appealing to the intended audience and effective within available distribution channels? How does Headquarters liaise with other organisations to ensure programme placement, distribution and viewer outreach?

These are daunting questions — complex for a UNICEF office anywhere. Project administration is often difficult, especially since UNICEF is not a broadcaster, nor are we an animation studio. UNICEF does not have in-house animation production capacity and backup distribution support.

But UNICEF does have a unique strength — a long and successful tradition in development communications. Social mobilisation activities relying heavily on the media have raised developing country immunisation rates to levels often exceeding those of industrialised countries. UNICEF's on-site field orientation has allowed the organisation to develop an expertise in meeting the daily requirements of children in need, whether that be in allocating emergency supplies, offering high level government planning assistance or in the realisation of radio and TV information and advocacy campaigns.

The implementation of animation in UNICEF programmes is important and timely. Never before in history have information technologies been so available to so many people. National television stations are multiplying, satellite services are pervasive, programming needs abound, and viewers are searching for relevant programming that will entertain and inform.

UNICEF and the Second Animation for Development Workshop

In November 1994, UNICEF, with the help of Walt Disney Feature Animation, hosted its Second Animation for Development Workshop and Summit in Orlando, Florida. The workshop was designed to bring UNICEF staff, world class animators, non-governmental organizations and animation business leaders together for the first time to enhance child survival and development through creative communication. This is exactly what happened. Over sixty-two countries were represented at the workshop and more than forty UNICEF field offices were in attendance. Animation industry leaders also answered the call, and the biggest names in international animation took part. Companies and organisations in attendance included: Atelier Camera Enfants Admis, ASIFA, Australia Children's Television Foundation, Cairo Cartoon Studio, Canal 3 (Guatemala), Children's Television Workshop, Colossal Pictures, Hanna-Barbera Cartoons, Jamaica Broadcasting Corporation, Mauricio de Sousa Productions, MTV, Namibia Broadcasting Corporation, National Film Board of Canada, National Film School of Denmark, Nickelodeon, Pakistan Television Corporation, Street Kids International, Television Suisse Romande, Turner Broadcasting, Walt Disney Feature Animation and Warner Brothers.

The workshop gave UNICEF staff an opportunity to look at the development and management implications of animation projects, and opened up the eyes of country offices to the possibilities of utilising this exciting art form. It gave UNICEF communicators a major networking opportunity with high level television and animation studio professionals and animators, who were inspired by the Workshop and who want to help form new alliances between the industry and UNICEF programmers.

The book you are about to read is a result of this Second Animation for Development Workshop and Summit. Most of the chapters within are taken directly from participants' presentations or keynote addresses. We've tried to include a broad sampling of issues concerning the use of animation for development communications from a number of different perspectives.

The first several chapters present an overview of animation, including a look at the history of animation by Disney historian Charles Solomon, entertainment programming for development from a UNICEF perspective, an alternative view of styles of animation from the president of ASIFA, a paper on formative research in the UNICEF/Hanna-Barbera animated initiative in South Asia entitled *Meena*, and views on animation on serious issues by Academy Award- winning animator John Canemaker. The next several chapters focus on specific issues concerning the "how to's" of animation, including merchandising ideas and products from the Walt Disney point of view; training animators; Children's Television Workshop and a non-profit model of communications, and the importance of listening to kids' perspectives by Nickelodeon President Geraldine Laybourne. The last portion of the book presents a number of case studies by a variety of authors on animation issues. Chapters include: pro-social animation by MTV Creative Director Abby Terkuhle, interactive CD-ROMs, low-cost computer animation, and an in-depth look at Turner Communications' environmental cartoon, *Captain Planet.*

Many of these chapters deal quite specifically with UNICEF issues or make reference to UNICEF projects. We believe that the information contained in this book can be utilised within a broad range of settings and can be incorporated into any development communications programme, and that the messages it contains are universal. We hope that the use of animation to communicate on social and health issues will continue to flourish as we near the year 2000 — and beyond. It is also our hope that as life-saving messages are increasingly disseminated using this exciting and accessible medium of communication, the number of childhood deaths from preventable causes will continue to decrease. After all, it is the goal of every development and aid organisation to eventually go out of business!

William Hetzer is Chief of the Radio, Television and Film Section of UNICEF New York's Division of Information.

Animation's Recent Past

Charles Solomon

Educational films will never replace the teacher. The three R's are basic (reading, 'riting, 'rithmetic), but their advancement by means of the motion picture screen will give more people in this world an opportunity to learn. Pictures can make both teaching and learning a pleasure. And educators argue that when a student has begun to learn and like it, half the problem is solved.

Walt Disney

In the beginning, there was magic. The viewers who bolted at the image of a moving train projected by the Lumiere Brothers in 1895, regarded the first experiments in film animation, beginning with J. Stuart Blackton's *Humorous Phases of Funny Faces* (1906), as magic, or something akin to it. The supernatural image of animation was reinforced by the use of stop-motion techniques to create such eerie effects as a loaf of bread slicing itself with a saw in the popular live action film, *The Haunted House* (1907). However, animation pioneer Winsor McCay was so annoyed when audiences assumed his first films were done using trick photography of live actors rather than sequences of drawings, he deliberately chose a character that couldn't be faked for his third film, the seminal *Gertie the Dinosaur* (1914).

Although their films were released by live-action studios, Blackton, McCay and a third important pioneer, Emile Cohl, did all the drawings for their films themselves. Animation entered a new phase when Raoul Barre opened the first animation studio in 1913 in New York City, just seven years after the creation of *Humorous Phases*. By 1918, there were a dozen studios operating in New York alone, turning out the silent shorts that helped to make animation synonymous with slapstick comedy to movie-goers.

But the use of animation for educational and propaganda purposes dates back nearly as far. The first feature-length animated film, Quirino Christiani's lost *El Apostle* (*The Apostle*, 1917) was a satire on the political situation in Argentina. During World War I, Max Fleischer, the future producer of the *Out of the Inkwell* and *Betty Boop* cartoons, made animated training films for the US Army. Enraged by the German attack on the Cunard liner Lusitania that occurred on May 7, 1915, Winsor McCay spent the next 22 months making 25,000 drawings for *The Sinking of the Lusitania* (1918), a dark, angry film that condemns the actions of "the Hun."

In 1923, Fleischer produced *Einstein's Theory of Relativity*, an hour-long educational film that combined live action, still artwork and simple animation, and it received favourable comments from Einstein himself. Walter Lantz blurred the line between entertainment and propaganda with *Confidence* (1933), a curious short, in which a singing caricature of Franklin D. Roosevelt explains to Oswald Rabbit that confidence is a magical cure for the Depression.

The Paris-based Czech artist, Barthold Bartosch, made animated films with social and political themes, culminating in *L'idee* (*The Idea*, 1932), based on a series of woodcuts by the Belgian artist Frans Masereel. The pro-Communist message and nude figures in the 30-minute film provoked a scandal that led to it being banned. Later in the 1930s, there was an attempt in Italy to produce an animated biography of Benito Mussolini, but the project was never completed. In Jonathan Swift's satire, *The New Gulliver* (1935), the first Soviet animated feature, puppet animator Alexander Ptushko infused Marxist dialects and a miners' strike against the corrupt aristocrats of Lilliput.

World War II gave great impetus to the use of animation for both educational and propaganda purposes. Studies conducted by the US military showed that troops learned difficult concepts faster, more easily and more enjoyably through animated films. The armed services commissioned thousands of animated training films from the Hollywood studios during the war years. In 1942-43, the Disney studio alone produced more than 204,000 feet of film, with 95 percent going to the military (prior to the war, the studio's greatest annual output amounted to 37,000 feet).

Some of the most talented animators in the industry joined the 18th Air Force Base Unit (First Motion Picture Unit) under Major Rudy Ising. Based at the old Hal Roach Studio in Los Angeles, a staff of between 125 and 150 officers, enlisted men and civilians produced the training film *Position Firing*, which proved so popular that soldiers at some bases preferred watching those antics to the Dinah Shore films that were also available in ten cent viewing machines.

At the same time, it became increasingly difficult to distinguish between entertainment and propaganda in Hollywood cartoons. Donald Duck encouraged Americans to pay the newly instituted income tax ("Taxes to beat the Axis") in *The New Spirit* (1943). Bugs Bunny outwitted the Japanese Imperial Navy in *Bugs Bunny Nips the Nips* (1944). In case audiences missed the caricature in Tex Avery's *The Blitz Wolf* (1942), a title card noted "Any similarity to that little %*@# Hitler is not coincidental." George Pal portrayed the Nazi Wehrmarcht as a goose-stepping troop of robots in *Tulips Shall Grow* (1943).

In 1943, Walt Disney produced his four most famous anti-Nazi shorts: *Reason and Emotion*, *Education for Death*, *Chicken Little* and the Oscar-winning *Der Fuehrer's Face*, which depicted Donald Duck as a reluctant worker in a German munitions plant. In August of that year, he released *Victory Through Airpower*, a feature-length adaptation of Major Alexander P. de Seversky's book advocating the superiority of air warfare over traditional tactics.

This mixing of animated entertainment and propaganda was by no means restricted to the United States. When John Grierson asked Norman McLaren to found an animation unit within the National Film Board of Canada (NFB) in 1942, its express purpose was "to explain Canada to Canadians and people of other nations." The imaginative films of the NFB were supposed to help tie together the country's ethnically and geographically diverse population. The first three Japanese animated features such as *Momotaro, The Brave Navy* (1943) *Momotaro, God's Soldier* (1944) and *Fukuchan and the Submarine* (1944) were propaganda films created at the request of the Imperial Navy.

The Old Lady's Camping Trip is a well-known film about fire prevention that combines hilarious antics with information on the do's and don'ts of camping.

In 1943, three former Disney artists, Stephen Bosustow, Dave Hilberman and Zachary Schwartz, organized the Industrial Film and Poster Service (IFPS) to produce materials for war industries. In 1944, the studio received a major commission from the United Auto Workers to produce *Hell-Bent for Election*, a re-election film for Franklin D. Roosevelt. Directed by Chuck Jones, this is a rare example of animation being used in an election campaign. As the IFPS expanded at the end of the war, the studio was reorganized as United Productions of America (UPA). The emphasis on limited movements and flatter, contemporary graphic styles that would transform the look of world animation during the 1950s, can be seen in such early works as *Flat Hatting*, part of the "Flight

Safety" series for the US Navy and *The Brotherhood of Man*, a film designed to facilitate the integration of the United Auto Workers' Union in the Southern US.

After the war, animation continued to be used to transmit difficult or abstract knowledge. In 1945, Disney began a series of educational shorts dealing with health issues for the Coordinator of Inter-American Affairs. *Hookworm* (1945), *Cleanliness Brings Health* (1945) and *How Disease Travels* (1945) explained basic hygiene to rural audiences in Latin America, while *Planning for Good Eating* (1946) focused on nutrition. The first British animated features *Handling Ships* (1946) and *Water for Fire-Fighting* (1949) were instructional films from the Halas and Batchelor studio, of which parts of the former film remain in use half a century later.

Walt Disney also produced a wide variety of didactic films for North American viewers, some of which were screened in schools, while others were shown in theatres or on television, including *Motor Mania* (1950), *How to have an Accident in the Home* (1956) and *Donald Duck in Mathmagic Land* (1959). John Southerland, a Disney alumnus, established a studio of his own to produce industrial films, many of which had a strong ideological bent.

Some of the most popular post-war animated educational films were made for The Bell Science Series, which was intended to counteract the negative image of scientists that the war had produced in America. Academy Award winner Frank Capra directed the first four entries in the series *Our Mr. Sun* (1956), *Hemo the Magnificent* (1956), *The Strange Case of the Cosmic Rays* (1957) and *The Unchained Goddess* (1958), which combined live- action footage with animation from the Shamus Culhane Studio. The Bell Telephone System underwrote the hour-long films and offered them free to school systems around the country. They stimulated the interest of thousands of baby boom-era children in various areas of science.

Norman McLaren won an Oscar for *Neighbours* (1952), and the National Film Board became one of the centres of creativity in world animation during the 1960s, 1970s and the 1980s. Artists from various countries produced films at the NFB, including educational films on subjects that ranged from the rights of the child (*Every Child*, 1979) to fire safety (*The Old Lady's Camping Trip*, 1983) and how to avoid accidents (*Every Dog's Guide to Home Safety*, 1986).

The Soviet-dominated regimes of postwar Eastern Europe underwrote film studios where animators enjoyed greater artistic freedom than their live action counterparts. Many Eastern European animated films from this era are thinly disguised political allegories. In *The Hand* (1965) by Czech puppet animator Jiri Trnka, a monstrous human hand forces a tiny sculptor to carve its portrait. Yugoslavian animator Borivoj Dovnikovic satirised the appeal of militarism in *The Flower Lover* (1970). In *Le Jeu des Anges* (*Game of Angels*, 1964) expatriate and Polish animator Walerian Borowczyk presented a chilling evocation of the Nazi death camps.

Small animation studios have been founded in several developing countries in recent decades. Although some animation was done in Cuba prior to World War II, several political propaganda films were made at the Instituto Cubano de Arte y Industria Cinematográficos, shortly after the Castro revolution, including *La prensa seria* (*The Serious Press*, 1960), *El tiburon y las sardinas* (*The Shark and the Sardines*, 1961), *La quema de la caña* (*The Fire of the Canefield*, 1961) and *Los Indocubanos* (1964), a study of the pre- Columbian peoples of Cuba.

In 1963, Mohamed Aram released the first Algerian animated film, *La fete de l'arbre* (*The Festival of Tree*), which invited viewers to replant forests destroyed during the war for independence. He followed this debut piece with two educational works, *Ah s'il savait lire* (*If He Knew How to Read*, 1963) about illiteracy, and *Les microbes des poubelles* (*The Germs in the Garbage Cans*, 1964) on urban sanitation. Elsewhere in Africa, the National Film and Television Institute of Ghana has produced a number of educational films since its establishment in 1980, including *Road Safety Campaign*, *Drug Abuse* and *Trees for Life*.

During the 1960s, a number of propaganda films were animated in North Vietnam, including *The Kitty* (1966) and *The Talking Blackbird* (1967), both directed by Ngo Manh Lan. Since unification, production has expanded to encompass both the northern and southern parts of the country. The Sri Lankian Television Training Institute has produced a few animated educational films, including *Health Through Hygiene* (1985) and *Environmental Protection* (1987). Most of the animated educational and propaganda films made in the developing world have been seen only by local audiences, although examples have screened at international festivals in recent years.

© National Film Board of Canada. Norman McLaren

A scene from Norman McLaren's *Neighbours*

The most successful use of animation to transmit information and alter opinions during the postwar era has occurred in the field of television commercials. Although animation accounts for only about five percent of the commercials broadcast at any given time, a disproportionately high percentage of the best-known and most honoured spots have been animated. Advertisers have exhibited the qualities that make animation so effective as a teaching tool. These include the ability to convey information more succinctly and remain fresh after repeated viewing.

Although commercial animation rarely receives the same respect as theatrical filmmaking, the demand for new, attention-getting visuals has enabled commercial animators to serve as intermediaries between *avant garde* and mainstream filmmakers. The most imaginative styles, innovative designs and new techniques appear in commercials before they're used by studio filmmakers. Computer graphics were used for commercials, networks logos, programme titles and station identification spots years before they appeared in such big-budget special effects features as *Terminator II* (1991) and *Jurassic Park* (1993), in the US.

Today, the use of animation to present information and sway opinions takes many forms. For example, rather than have an actor describe the use of fossil DNA in *Jurassic Park*, Stephen Spielberg had the Kurtz and Friends Studio animate an anthropomorphized strand of DNA. A short film about DNA appears on the prototype ride, explaining the origin of the dinosaur park. A recipient of a John D. and Catherine T. MacArthur Grant, James Blinn created simple computer-generated images for educational programmes about physics and advanced mathematics. Graphs, equations, symbols, and cartoon figures elucidate abstract concepts, including Einstein's Theory of Relativity. In 1988, director Stephen Johnson and producer Prudence Fenton coordinated the work of 42 animators from around the world, who did sequences illustrating the 30 articles of the Universal Declaration of Human Rights issued by the United Nations. The 19-minute film was shown between acts on the Amnesty International Human Rights tour that featured musicians Bruce Springsteen, Peter Gabriel, Tracy Chapman and Sting.

The possibilities are endless: Ninety years after the premiere of *Humorous Phases Of Funny Faces,* the magic remains.

Charles Solomon, an internationally respected critic and historian of animation, is the author of *Enchanted Drawings: The History of Animation* and *The Disney That Never Was.*

Suggestions for Further Reading

Bendazzi, Giannalberto. *Cartoons: One Hundred Years of Cinema Animation.* Bloomington, IA: Indiana University Press, 1994.

Crafton, Donald. *Before Mickey: The Animated Film 1989-1928.* Cambridge, MA: The MIT Press, 1982.

Diamant, Lincoln. *Television's Classic Commercials: The Golden Years 1948-1958.* New York: The Hastings House, 1971.

Shale, Richard. *Donald Duck Joins Up: The Walt Disney Studio During World War II.* Ann Arbor, MI: The UMI Press, 1982.

Shull, Michael S. & Wilt, David E. *Doing Their Bit: Wartime American Short Films, 1939- 1945.* Jefferson, NC: McFarland & Co., 1987.

Solomon, Charles. *Enchanted Drawings: The History of Animation.* New York: Wing Books, 1994.

SECTION ONE

How to Animate?

The Animated Film in Development Communication

George McBean & Neill McKee

The Past

The *International Encyclopedia of Communications* says: " A great deal of the history of the West since the end of the fifteenth century seems intimately connected to the spread of printed books. But definition of that connection is far from simple. It has, for instance, been proposed that the reproducible illustrations that printed books contain and disseminate, are a far more significant factor in the retention and spread of scientific and technical knowledge than their texts. Such a suggestion is not far fetched. The difficulties that might face a botanist, an engineer or an architect using books with no illustrations at all . . . are obvious."

This paragraph highlights the significance of the visual image in the spread of knowledge since the fifteenth century, when the world's total population was a mere 500 million. If we take it a step further, we can envisage the difficulties a non-literate mother or father today may have in trying to retain health or development information. If we compare the power of the printed illustration with the potential of television images, we can see the potential for sharing information on an unprecedented scale.

Below is the first of 17 drawings used to create this short flip sequence which takes you to the chapter on research for the Meena series. These drawings are taken from the episode *Dividing the Mango.*

© UNICEF, animation by Ram Mohan

The Present

Today, we can marvel at the assortment of available information technologies. Yet even in this media-rich environment, certain types of information are more effectively disseminated through visual images. Satellite pictures of the earth provide us with details of weather, vegetation and crops. Video cameras seek international news stories or provide security in banks and elsewhere. People in the rural villages of developing countries can see what American homes look like from television sitcoms. Science uses animated images to show the public how a black hole in space functions. Lawyers use animation to reconstruct an accident or crime to help a jury quickly visualise what took place, rather than take up valuable court time on lengthy verbal explanations.

Although the variety of information techniques is impressive, their application is still limited, especially in the dissemination of health and development information. There are many examples of how animation explains space stations, but none to show a non-literate mother how to rehydrate her dying baby. An African farmer's crop failure may show up clearly on a satellite photo, but there is no sophisticated visual aid to explain to him what could have been done to prevent a bad harvest.

Today there are almost 950 million non-literate people on the planet. Many still have not felt the positive effects of illustration, let alone visual technology — it is common to find classrooms throughout the developing world with no visual materials on the wall and just a few poor quality illustrations in books. In many countries, the art of drawing and illustrating itself has been sadly relegated to a recreational activity.

The Future

It is estimated that well into the next millennium there will still be large numbers of non-literate people (more than 1 billion). This statistic is especially alarming when you consider that there is a definite link between parental literacy and child mortality. The difficulty of conveying child survival and health messages to people who are illiterate is not insurmountable — there are ways of passing information that does not involve reading. Without decreasing attempts to spread literacy skills, there are now greater opportunities to present information in a way that pre-literate people can understand.

The number of television sets now exceeds 1 billion, with an audience three to four times this figure. If the urban child of the present is representative, the child of the future will spend more time in his or her formative years watching cartoons on television than they will at college. It may be some years before the computer, which offers even greater potential for education, becomes a household item in the homes of the poorest sectors of the developing world. Today, television is fast establishing itself as the most widespread source of visual information.

The potential for partnerships between those who have expertise in gathering information and those who have skills in disseminating information has already begun to manifest itself in the business sector. Advances in the development of CD-ROM have brought together teams of information specialists, including writers, musicians and animators, to create learning materials that use a broad range of presentation skills in a single format. This sort of creative partnership in the social sector is long overdue.

Since current figures estimate that eighty percent of childhood deaths in developing countries are preventable, it appears that creating better health is really more of a communications challenge than a medical one. Given the ability of animators to present information clearly and accurately in an entertaining way, it could be argued that the skills of the animator are as important to the future of the developing world as those of the doctor.

Creating a Communications Symbol

Animated film characters can create communications symbols that can be identified regionally or even worldwide. Who does not know Mickey Mouse, Donald Duck or Yogi Bear? These characters have entertained generations of people. They are instantly recognised and are associated with laughter and relaxation.

Animated communication symbols have already been used successfully around the world to focus on development issues and to support social movements. In the 1950s, animated films on health issues like malaria were used extensively in health education programmes around the world. *Prescription for Health*, a 1983 film on water and sanitation produced by Canada's International Development Research Centre, has been adapted for use in over thirty languages and is used in UNICEF-supported programmes extensively throughout the developing world. In the late 1980s, Street Kids International produced *Karate Kids*, a film on street children and AIDS prevention, which was highly effective in communicating resistance skills to many underprivileged children and raising international awareness of their plight.

Also in the 1980s, UNICEF used animated films at community viewing centres in Nepal and found them to be extremely useful in explaining health information to non-literate, rural audiences. At night in open air venues, these films were often projected onto a white cloth hanging on a tree. Men would watch on one side of the cloth while women would view the reverse image on the other. A presenter would articulate the voices of the characters on a loudspeaker. The Nepalese audiences would talk for weeks afterwards about the issues portrayed in the film.

Participants at the animation workshop in Nepal in 1987.

It was in Nepal that UNICEF first became involved in training animators. UNICEF staff had observed that Nepalese artists used styles in their traditional Thangka paintings that could easily be translated to animation. Similar to animation production, the Thangka was passed along a production line with one artist outlining the image, another painting in the Buddha, and yet another background artist adding the scenery. This sparked the idea that the considerable skills and traditional methods of local artists could be easily transferred to animation.

In 1987, a workshop was held in Kathmandu. UNICEF approached a group of local Nepalese artists and invited them to be trained in a style of animation that was suitable to their established skills.

Meanwhile, two Czechoslovakian animators were commissioned to run the workshop. Afterwards, four Nepalese artists were invited to Kratky Film Studios in Prague for six months of animation training. Upon completion, the artists returned to Nepal where they now run a small studio and work closely with several development agencies to produce animated films for the local market.

In March 1990, UNICEF, in cooperation with Kratky Film, organised the first international seminar on "film animation for development" in Prague. Some 120 participants from 49 countries explored different ways of using animation to disseminate health and development messages to parents and children. At the conclusion of the Prague seminar, two of the world's leading animation studios, Walt Disney Feature Animation and Hanna-Barbera Cartoons, pledged to assist UNICEF in its development communication efforts. Links were later established between UNICEF and Children's Television Workshop, the creators of *Sesame Street*, to develop future collaborations in developing countries.

As a result of the Prague conference, a number of animation initiatives were launched worldwide, including:

•The Meena Communication Initiative on the Girl Child in South Asia was created in cooperation with Lightbox Motion Pictures, Bombay, Hanna-Barbera Cartoons and their subsidiary, Fil-Cartoons, Manila. This initiative has led to the production of animated films on issues such as education, income generation, nutrition, workload, early marriage, son preference, and water and sanitation as they relate to the girl child.

•The Maximo animation project in Ecuador, in cooperation with Disney Feature Animation, has produced films on health issues, such as immunisation, oral rehydration therapy and iodine deficiency disorders. The life-saving messages in the films are communicated by a colourful and friendly toucan named Maximo.

•The Caribbean Area Initiative in cooperation with Walt Disney Feature Animation and Brazilian animator Walbercy Ribas, has now produced seven animated films on the subjects of safe motherhood, early childhood development and life skills, as well as public service announcements on child abuse, measles, teenage pregnancy and children with HIV.

•Cooperation between Children's Television Workshop, Televisa, and UNICEF Mexico has resulted in a series of *Sesame Street* programmes (*Plaza Sésamo*) on children's health and development issues in Latin America, with a component of animated film in the programmes.

•Cuban animators have produced several television spots focusing on relevant UNICEF issues.

Entertainment and Education

The impact of animation on development is strongest when it entertains as well as educates. According to John Hopkins University's Centre for Communication Programmes, it must be "personal, popular and persuasive" to do so. Through entertainment, we can appeal to the emotions that drive people's decisions and strike deeply into the value systems upon which our lives are built.

Mixing social and health messages with entertainment is difficult. As social communicators, our work is often driven by the supposed imperative of "getting the message out." Too often, programme formats, posters and other materials contain too many messages, drowning the intended audience with so much information that the material becomes ineffective and communication does not occur. It is imperative that programme managers realise that for information to be cost effective, it must be packaged in a motivational way, as information by itself can seldom empower people who have little resources or formal education.

Using Animated Film to Communicate Sensitive Issues

Another major asset of animation is its facility to communicate sensitive issues without alienating audiences. One of the most difficult concepts to communicate is information about the spread of diseases. In North America and Europe, disease theory as the basis of public health measures only became popular in the mid-1800s. In developing countries, where universal primary education still remains a challenge, disease theory is often perceived as unbelievable. Communicating the concept that the overload of faeces in the environment is responsible for ill health and child death is difficult, because through religious and traditional values, most people see themselves as "clean." Telling them that faecal matter is getting into their mouths through their hands, food and other vectors is a sensitive matter.

Besides such sensitive health issues, other social issues can be tackled through animated messages. In the Meena Communication Initiative in South Asia, the heroine of a series of animated films produced by UNICEF is an empowered girl who uses her intelligence to remain in school and to solve many problems for her family, friends and community. The initiative is a major breakthrough in view of the position in society that most women and girls hold in the northern belt of South Asia. The girl child in the region is discriminated against from birth.

© UNICEF

Images of Meena can be seen on the streets of Dhaka, Bangladesh.

UNICEF is addressing yet more sensitive issues in Eastern and Southern Africa with animated film. In this region, adolescent girls are five times more likely to be HIV positive than adolescent boys — a manifestation of a social construction which relegates girls to an inferior position, beginning at birth and continuing through their formative years. Parents prefer sons and often treat girls as those "who are just passing through," and their unequal proportion of household chores puts a heavy burden on them and adversely affects their education. As they grow older, they are often sexually harassed and abused by their male peers and by older men. Low self esteem, poor communication and lack of problem solving skills lead girls to teenage pregnancy and early marriage. Their options for the future are limited and few escape the spiral.

Animated Film and Cross-Cultural Communication

Live action film on social issues can have the disadvantage of being distant from all but a very specific ethnic group. Audiences of low visual literacy or lower educational background may be more fascinated with the context of the message (the clothes people are wearing, the houses they live in), than the message itself. While live action film gives people a broader world view, its attempt to communicate social issues may fail. The audience may reject the message, assuming that it does not apply to their own ethnic group.

Animated film, on the other hand, communicates across cultural boundaries. The work of Disney, Hanna-Barbera and others has universal appeal. They are watched and loved by children and adults around the world. The Meena character appeals to people all over Asia, not just the region for which it was designed, and has attracted attention in Europe and North America for utilisation in development education. Through proper research, animated film characters, backgrounds and storylines can be tailored to strike a common chord of cultural identity, which can expose problems and propose solutions across a whole region or population.

Since animated film is expensive, regional rather than local animation projects make sense. Until the cost of producing animated films is reduced by the growth and accessibility of computerised systems, programmes that appeal to single culture may not be cost effective. While a large country like India or China could produce cost effective animation, it may not make sense for countries like Mozambique, Lesotho or Somalia with a smaller audience reach.

One can even make a case for global animation projects, although there is still a debate as to whether animated film can have a truly global appeal and impact in communicating social issues. Global characters and stories may have great educational value, but for behavioural change and development, we may have to appeal to common cultural values with common cues. Making animated film too abstract in an attempt to create a universal appeal faces the same problems as live action footage. People may not identify with the problem or the solution proposed. They may be fascinated and amused by the moving figures, but reject the relevance of the messages themselves.

Extending the Reach: The Multimedia Imperative

Today, satellite television, cable-user groups, video theatres and clubs, community viewing facilities, access to neighbourhood televisions, mobile film and video facilities, non-governmental organisations and religious networks, and other informal channels, are available to growing numbers of people. Very often we find that remote villagers and people in poor urban areas have somehow managed to see popular programming.

It must be acknowledged that in many regions of the world it will be many years before people have easy, regular access to film and television. It is therefore important that animated film and video productions should not be the only means of "enter-educating," but should be part of an integrated approach. There are many media through which the same stories and messages can be communicated — comic books, magazine comic strips, illustrated storybooks, posters, learning games, child-to-child activity sheets, radio programmes and audio cassettes. In addition, facilitator guidelines can be designed for use in group processes, with or without the film. The programme's reach can be extended through the popularization of themes through drama groups, theme songs, and marketing of products such as dishware, clothing, school supplies, dolls, games, stickers, activity books, calendars and greeting cards.

Merchandising animated symbols can be a profitable way to generate funds and a useful tool for advocacy. The merchandising of animated heroes and heroines has proven very successful for the major animation studios. Development agencies can take advantage of this potential, especially in countries with a large middle class population. Revenue generated from such sales can contribute to development projects or go into a revolving fund to begin or sustain production of a new series.

The priorities of the social communication programme become much more widely known through a multimedia approach. If we can reach the decision-makers through the popularisation of entertaining solutions, the job of reaching the people for whom the programme is designed is made that much easier. To this end, UNICEF must build alliances in the development and use of communication packages with government agencies, NGOs, service clubs, children's clubs, scouts and guides, artists, entertainers and others. In this way, animation symbols can become the communication medium in a social movement for education and development.

Animation and Behaviour Development Programming

In order for people to change to more positive behaviours, they must first be motivated. The animated film with its high entertainment value has a great potential to do this. Through in-depth formative research, which uncovers the values, attitudes and beliefs of the target audience, programming can be constructed with storylines that are both informative and motivational; appealing to cultural roots and to emotions which catalyse change.

However, we should not stop there. Information and motivation are necessary, but not enough. Programming must also address the ability of people to act. Educational packages should be designed to train people in new technical, physical, cognitive and psycho-social skills. Stories designed around an animated character can be created to assist in the acquisition of skills, such as problem solving, critical thinking, negotiating, communicating, coping with stress, self- assessment and self-awareness.

Positive behaviour change and development must happen in an enabling environment with supportive peers, family, and community services, as well as with the support of appropriate policy and legislation. When a multimedia and multi-partner approach is used in prioritising issues, the environment will foster positive, permanent change. A popular and compelling set of stories that is conveyed in an entertaining way and is rooted in the culture of the region can help to soften the debate. Raising sensitive issues in a lateral way rather than head-on, decreases the chances of resistance. This power to communicate sensitive issues without alienating audiences is a major asset of animation.

Cost Advantages of Animated Film

Animation can be expensive, especially labour-intensive full-cel film, which requires up to 10,000 individual pictures to be drawn and painted for just a 12-minute episode. The advent of computerised systems has cut costs. For example, today line drawings are being increasingly transferred to a computer system for colouring and finishing, considerably reducing costs. However, there is still no alternative to the art of hand-drawn animation when natural movement is required. In many places, there are few or no resources and facilities to support an animation industry. So at the moment, we are faced with a relatively painstaking and expensive production process.

Despite the initial expense, there are cost advantages to animation. Animated film hardly dates at all. Many of the original animated segments for *Sesame Street* are still in use today, 20 years after their production. Cartoons produced 30 to 40 years ago can still be seen and enjoyed today. If programmes are produced to address issues that will be a problem for some time, these films will likely remain current for as many as 25 years. In comparison, the average shelf life for live action documentaries is perhaps five to seven years. After this, clothing styles and other cues set the film in a context and time frame and makes the message less effective.

Another major cost benefit of animated film is the ease in which language versions can be produced. A well-researched and well-projected film can be dubbed into many languages. Audiences allow a greater latitude in lip sychronisation in animation than in live action films. This means films can be used in a wide region and greatly reduces the actual cost per language version.

Conclusion

The new spirit of animation for development seems to have sprouted initiatives in all corners of the world, forging alliances between the public and private sectors. UNICEF and its partners must consolidate the lessons learned from previous communication initiatives, and endeavour to incorporate capacity building and sustainablity into new communication programmes. The future of animation for development communication and education will be very bright if we can rapidly set up the institutional facilitating mechanisms that allow our buds to blossom. Ultimately, the measure of our success will be the empowerment and betterment of the world's children. Animation provides the world means, so therefore it is to these goals we must now strive.

George McBean is a cartoonist and the Communications Officer for UNICEF's Caribbean Area Office.

Neill McKee is the Senior Programme Communications Officer for UNICEF's Eastern and Southern Africa Regional Office and the author of *Social Mobilization and Social Marketing in Developing Communities.*

Entertainment Programming for Development

Warren Feek

© UNICEF

In Bukina Faso, the radio acts as an important source of information.

The UNICEF Approach: New Partners and Processes

Entertaining and being entertained are activities that consume the attention and time of substantial proportions of the world's population. One only has to consider the devotion of people to their favourite television soap opera or radio play, or the effort that communities put into creating and performing music and drama for local audiences and for national events. Animation, from hand puppets to computer animation, is an important part of the entertainment process. A Senegalese poet who spends his or her time performing in local villages and a Hollywood producer of action movies may seem different, but essentially, they perform the same role. They are both trying to entertain and influence. They are part of what is referred to as the entertainment industry.

The process of entertainment, which not only amuses people but engages, informs and stimulates them, can be a vital aspect of development programmes that need to encourage discussion and dialogue, provoke peer support, provide basic information in an effective way and create a more supportive environment for the furtherance of youth health. In this chapter I will place animation in its broader context, both as an essential element of entertainment and as an example of how all forms of entertainment can be mobilised in pursuit of UNICEF's goals. In making those connections, I will refer to the devastating impact that youth related health problems, including HIV / AIDS and teenage pregnancy, will have on achieving reductions in infant, child and maternal mortality.

Entertaining for Change: A Long Standing Tradition

All cultures have popular forms of entertainment which excite, interest, please and sometimes provoke, such as the human or shadow puppets of Indonesia, wandering dance and drama troupes in Africa, the Mariachi musicians in Mexico and the action songs of the Pacific. As Alfonso Gumucio-Dagron points out in his recent book on popular theatre, "entertainment has been married to education since its inception. There is virtually no experience of popular theatre in the world that has not been related to an educational process." The Indonesian puppets provide an example of this. *wayang orang* (human puppets), *wayang golek* (puppet dolls), *ketprak* (traditional Javanese drama) and *ludruk* (humorous drama) have, as part of their traditional form, conveyed messages on health, education and politics. A recent study by the Family Health Services Project in Lagos and Johns Hopkins University Population Communications Services makes the same observation for another part of the world:

> "African communities have a strong tradition of communicating through entertainment. Fireside chats are a cherished part of many rural evenings. Proverbs, skits, songs, dances and drama are...used to teach younger generations about customs and traditions."

Traditionally, the process of entertaining has been key to the distribution of news, the fomenting of political change, the mobilisation of social action, the continuance of cultural practice and the challenging of detrimental practices. People wishing to consolidate power and influence have sought to influence the entertainers. Change through entertainment or adversely, the thwarting of change through the control of the entertainment industry, is a long standing phenomenon. These struggles reflect the power and influence of the process. To increase our chances of reaching child survival and development goals, UNICEF and other relevant agencies at national and international levels should seek to expand our work with the entertainment industry.

Technology provides the opportunity to work with the entertainment industry on both national and global scales in order to influence countries, communities and individuals to take actions that will ensure child survival and achieve further reductions in infant, child and maternal mortality. This can be done through a number of entertainment media — soap operas, which are an established part of life for many communities, music and music videos, and the enormous film and television industries, especially in cities such as Bombay, Cairo, Mexico City and Hong Kong. Animation, thanks to companies such as Disney, is now a universal form of entertainment that is not just popular but also provides stimulating and thought-provoking approaches to sensitive social issues.

The transmission of visual images through video, film and television is rapidly increasing. Statistics on television viewership are startling. As *The Economist* has observed, "Since 1980, the number of television sets has almost tripled to nearly 1 billion . . . and ownership of sets will rise by five percent per year until the year 2000." The old argument that television is only for the elite is rapidly becoming obsolete. Allied to the increase in the numbers of television sets is the growth in popularity of video cassette recorders (VCRs). At the end of 1990, there were an estimated 200 million homes worldwide with VCRs and their number was steadily growing.

Sustainable Programming: The Need for Individual and Social Change

There are those who would ask: "Why should development organisations wish to use this opportunity?" After all, one can't immunise children, administer ORT, provide clean water or iodise salt through a mass communication process. Isn't communications really best for advocacy, fund raising and profile enhancement? This very limited view of the potential use of communications programming is one we hear all too often.

Achievement of child survival and development goals, including the enhancement of those programmes which address issues such as HIV/AIDS and other youth health concerns, requires changes in individual behaviour and detrimental social norms. This calls for a method of communication which can share knowledge and at the same time act as the primary vehicle for suggesting, encouraging, debating and reinforcing changes in individual behaviour, encouraging social norms and values that are positive for child health.

This communication can be utilised in the traditional areas of UNICEF concern. To give some examples: the life-saving remedy Oral Rehydration Therapy (ORT) may be widely available, but if people don't use it, children will continue to die of dehydration. To use ORT requires a change in behaviour. Increasing the prevalence of breast-feeding involves not just a behavioural change for many women, but most importantly a change in the culture to the acceptance of breast-feeding as important, legitimate and valuable. The same is true for the education of girls. If girls' enrolment in school is to increase in a sustainable way, there must be a distinct cultural and social change in the ways girls are perceived and treated.

The emerging issues that significantly challenge our ability to achieve child survival and development goals for the year 2000 provide even starker evidence for the need to address social and behavioural change through mass communications. Potential health problems related to sexuality and substance abuse will have a significant and long-standing impact on the chances of reaching child survival and development targets. A recent US Bureau of Census survey of sixteen developing countries showed that HIV/AIDS will dramatically reverse the previously positive trend of reductions in infant and child mortality. Many countries will return to Under Five Mortality Rates (U5MR) levels very close to or above the 1990 base figure.

Among the other health challenges is the emerging evidence from numerous countries that approximately forty percent of maternal mortality occurs in very young mothers. Changes in sexual habits will therefore become a UNICEF programming priority to reverse this trend. Another potential health problem, in an era in which there is increasing pressure and expectation for communities to fund their own health care, is the purchasing and use of tobacco and alcohol, representing not only a health cost, but an opportunity cost. For example, in some countries, household spending on alcohol is five times higher than spending on child health.

These sexual health and substance abuse issues pose the most difficult problems in terms of changing personal behaviour and social norms. There are no "quick-fix" solutions, and this extremely sensitive area requires education, debate, dialogue, the challenging of traditional practices, and giving a voice to the views and opinions of the younger generation. The course of personal and social change can be greatly facilitated through the use of entertainment in partnership with the entertainment industry.

Street children in Brazil

Focus

Many UNICEF field offices are beginning to utilise development communications as a means for enabling them and their partners to approach youth health issues in an effective manner. Some of the emerging principles for action include:

Fuel debate and discussion

Fuelling debate is the essence of behaviour and social change. In Cote d'Ivoire, UNICEF works with the national radio service to produce a programme that targets young people, broadcast from a small village to a national audience. Young people in the village are involved in a range of activities that encourage them to discuss their own views on sexual health issues and their position in society, and young people all over the country can share their experience.

Open minds to new ideas

This can be done by utilising the natural preference for entertainment. In the Honduran city of San Pedro Sula, UNICEF works with local partners to manage a communications centre called Comvida. This facility, through the use of entertainment communications, provides assistance to local groups wishing to discuss sexual issues, share relevant information, and propose changes in the way their community deals with such concerns.

Compel people to watch

This can be achieved through high-quality communication. In South Africa, UNICEF is one of a number of organisations working with local groups to produce an integrated approach to health communications. A television drama called *Soul City*, accompanied by radio dramas, newspaper inserts and an information booklet, cover a wide range of child and sexual health issues. The quality and format of their presentations has seen these programmes top the audience ratings. The resulting popularity means that such programmes are a topic of discussion in everyday life.

Utilise people's own interpretations

People's own perspectives are what is most important. In Brazil, an organisation works with young people, including street youth, to produce entertaining television programmes that reflect young people's views on sexual health issues. The programmes are shown in community plazas and on national television to stimulate debate on appropriate responses to a range of sexual health issues.

Sustain attention

This can be done through good music, good plots and attractive characters. In Uganda,

Straight Talk, a newspaper and radio series produced by young people, focuses on sexual health issues. Using an entertaining format designed to appeal to their peers, young people raise a number of issues relating to sexual health problems and suggest appropriate responses. Since the programme's style is youthful and entertaining, it sustains audience attention, gaining credibility and thereby the power to influence.

Programming: Maximising the Impact

How do we respond to the challenge of best utilising the programming opportunities presented by mass entertainment communication? By its very nature, the mass communications industry is a difficult spool to unwind. The creative process is fiercely independent. Writers, directors, filmmakers, musicians, actors and animators have no desire to be the mouthpiece for any special interest groups. There are control or direction forces — either from the State which owns the mass communication interest, or from the advertisers and others who pay. Both this independence and this control present obstacles. What can we do to overcome them?

There are several strategic options for the pursuit of child survival and development goals through the use of entertainment education. UNICEF can simply produce its own entertainment programmes to serve its interests and fundraise for the costs involved. The Meena Communication Initiative, which began in UNICEF Bangladesh as a way to emphasise and promote girl-child issues, is an excellent example of this approach, with impressive results. UNICEF staff, with assistance from Hanna-Barbera and their Philippine-based studio Fil-Cartoons, developed the project, raised the resources, brought together the research and production teams, and marketed the results to national broadcasters in the region.

We can work in partnership with established mass communication and entertainment organisations to develop mutually beneficial products. This partnership would most likely involve providing some funds and technical assistance to the outside organisations. The *Plaza Sésamo* initiative in conjunction with the Children's Television Workshop and Televisa in Mexico is an excellent example of this approach. UNICEF provided a platform for action and technical and financial assistance for the development of a new Latin American version of *Sesame Street*. *Plaza Sésamo* includes a substantial focus on child health issues.

Another option is to work with scriptwriters, producers and others responsible for putting together major media initiatives on youth health. There is a natural connection with these people, as often the most popular entertainment focuses on relationships, sex, family life, violence and gender relations. Those responsible for such programming often welcome, and sometimes seek, technical advice to ensure that they are dealing with sensitive subjects in an appropriate way. The provision of such advice is a window for influence.

In deciding how to pursue future communications goals, it is important to consider the capacity of the mass communications infrastructure in the individual country and the sensitivity of the specific issues being addressed. The tables in this chapter provide instruments for assessing the programming opportunities in countries and considering the opportunities for action. The questions in the brief situation analysis and the programming suggestions are derived from the experiences of UNICEF country offices working with partners in the mass communications industry.

If we are to be successful in ensuring that entertainment communication, including animation, is a more central component of UNICEF's programme approach, we need to argue the case in UNICEF terms. The criterion for this is: "Does it work?" There is a growing body of evidence for the impact of entertainment on social development goals. The Centre for Communication Programming at Johns Hopkins University has been to the fore in evaluating and providing this evidence.

One example of the impact of education on social development is the *Soul City* initiative in South Africa. The initiative involves health promotion through television and radio drama, newspapers inserts, a booklet and a public relations campaign and has achieved impressive results. *Soul City* has reached large numbers of people and has substantially raised the knowledge levels of the population on key child and youth health issues. A significant percentage of people reported changing their behaviour as a result of the entertaining programmes. The television and radio programmes became a hot topic of conversation in the home, community and workplace. This is a clear indication that the use of entertainment programming to achieve social goals works.

So, if such programming does work, can it help us progress towards UNICEF's goals for the year 2000? If these goals are to be achieved, they will require extensive communication of information to raise knowledge levels as well as changes in social norms to support individual and community action. Mass communication and entertainment can encourage this process. Radio and television programmes, traditional drama, music and dance that has already captured the attention and interest of populations is probably the most effective way to convey information on key health issues.

The achievement of child survival and development goals will depend on changes in social norms. For example, in order to achieve goals related to the education of girls, community attitudes relating to girls will need to change. Attitudes towards safe sex will have to change if goals concerning the reduction of HIV / AIDS cases and teenage pregnancies are to be attained. If women have no say in the nature of health services which are designed to meet their needs, real change is required to involve them in those decision-making processes. Communication in general and entertainment in particular can help foster debate and provide the rationale for changing social attitudes and beliefs.

UNICEF's *modus operandi* is to build partnerships and alliances for child survival and development. This is the next factor which we need to consider — can UNICEF mobilise influential partners by working in entertainment communications? Will this add to our list of allies, advocates and actors? Of course it will. The fast growing entertainment industry provides an opportunity for new partnerships. In the beginning of this chapter I quoted the dollar figure spent on entertainment in the last year. Our potential partners are spending that money, and many of them are after the same target audience as we are (children and young people) and focus on similar issues (health, sex, relationships and gender).

Women in discussion in Benin.

Finally, will the utilisation of entertainment communications to achieve social goals help us to reach worldwide audiences? Naturally! The very essence of mass communication and entertainment is global. There is no quicker way to reach people.

In Conclusion

The information and arguments above are made in order to provide broad rationale for UNICEF increasing its use of mass communications as an integral and valued part of its programmes on child, youth and women's survival and development. Animation has provided a glimpse of how to do this effectively and it will continue to open our eyes and minds to the possibilities that all forms of entertainment have in impacting the lives of children, young people and women.

Warren Feek works in the Health Promotion Unit in UNICEF New York to mobilise action in the use of mass communications for health promotion.

Situation Analysis: Mass Communications for Youth Health

MASS COMMUNICATION CAPACITY

Reach and Appeal

- Percentage of general population with access to/regularly use electronics (e.g. Radio, TV, movies, video), Print (e.g. newspapers, magazines) and traditional (e.g. theatre, music). Percentage of 10 to 24 population with access to/regularly use electronic (e.g. Radio, TV, movies, video), Print (e.g. newspapers, magazines) and traditional (e.g. theatre, music).
- Five most popular specific mass communication programmes/publications/initiatives—electronic, print, traditional—with general population.
- Five most popular specific mass communication programmes/publications/initiatives—electronic, print, traditional—with 10 to 24 year olds.
- Literacy rates—population and 10 to 24 year olds?
- Coverage of electronic, print and traditional mass communications—by geography, by gender, by income?

Capacity Indicators

- Quality of equipment used by radio, TV, newspaper and movie organisations?
- Standard of training of mass communicators?
- Quality of programme making?
- Trends in overall listening/reading/viewing/attending—for youth and the general population.
- Comparison of popularity of locally produced versus imported entertainment and news programmes and publications.
- Listener reactions to quality of programmes aired, shows attended and materials printed?
- Levels of interest/skill among mass communicators on women and youth health issues?
- Quality of information aired, shown or produced on women and youth health issues?
- Capacity for interactive programmes—e.g. talk shows, phone-ins, outside broadcasts, etc.—on sensitive youth health issues?
- Capacity to support young men and women expressing their perspectives through mass communication channels.

SOCIAL ENVIRONMENT FOR YOUTH

Youth Health Issues

- Average age of first sexual experience and trend with implications for women's health?
- Percentage and number of teenage pregnancies, trend in age of mother at first birth, implications for maternal/child mortality?
- HIV/AIDS infections with implications for infant and child mortality and numbers of orphans?
- Consumption trends for alcohol and tobacco with direct health implications and economic consequences, including capacity of households to purchase child health care?
- Usage by young people of family planning services.
- Trends in other STDs—with implications for women, child and youth health.
- Trends in violent behaviour with implications for women, children and young people?
- Usage by young people of health care facilities.
- Extent of youth involvement in managing (community) health care facilities.

Social Environment Indicators

- Legislation on youth health issues.
- Views on youth health issues by:
  - political leaders
  - traditional leaders
  - religious leaders
  - women's organisations
  - youth organisations
  - young people
- Tone of coverage of these issues in media?
- Cultural context for these issues—e.g. any taboos?
- Extent and nature of household discussion between young people and their elders on youth health issues.
- Extent and nature of discussion amongst young people and their peers on youth health issues.
- Youth behaviours causing most public concern?
- Stigma associated with women and/or youth health issues.
- Priority assigned by government to women and youth health issues—as indicated by trends in the budget allocations?

Summary of Strategic Options for Action with Partners

GENERALLY SUPPORTIVE SOCIAL ENVIRONMENT FOR YOUTH HEALTH

Strategic Options	*Extensive Mass Communications*	*Emerging Mass Communications*
Monitoring	Support mass communicators reporting on youth health status.	Monitor changes to the mass communication scene and their implications.
Training	Train young people to work with mass communicators.	Train mass communicators in communication for youth health.
Policy Advocacy	Support young people's involvement in mass communication policy debates.	Forum for discussion of mass communication policies for youth health promotion.
Direct Support	Comprehensive work encouraging makers of popular entertainment programmes to introduce youth health theme.	Specific support to one or two high profile mass communication for health programmes that will set the standard.
Networks	Establish regular communication system with mass communication people.	Form a network of mass communication people with an interest in youth health issues.
Recognition	Establish a "Youth Health and Mass Communications" award.	Initiate a "Young Communicator of the Year on Health" award.
Product Development	Support one or two programmes that demonstrate ground breaking approaches for young people to express their perspectives and ideas.	Broker relationships between local producers, writers and artists and internationally renowned production organisations.

Serious Fun: Animating Sensitive and Serious Issues

John Canemaker

When most people think of the animated film, images of comedic cats, mice, and rabbits come easily to mind, as do treasured memories of fairy tale heroes, heroines, witches and other villains. For nearly a century the animation industry has entertained the world with a pantheon of marvellous characters performing in traditional narratives.

But animation's role is not just to entertain. It also has great power as a teaching tool. Animation has the unique ability to take on difficult, complex matters in imaginative and entertaining ways that are beyond the capability of live action. This alternative use of animation remains a largely unexplored arena of opportunity for both designers and directors. Among the first pioneers in this arena are filmmakers John and Faith Hubley, who have inspired many filmmakers in this art. John once wrote about the alternative animation I describe above as an art whose purpose is to "increase awareness, to warn, to humanise, to elevate vision, to suggest goals, to deepen our understanding of ourselves and our relationships with each other."

When I think of animation, I see cancer treatments for children, advertisements for AIDS benefits, visual discussions about teen suicide, John Lennon's assassination and the fear of nuclear war. I see the use of abstract symbols to depict the inner workings of the imagination and the creative process, expressionistic explorations of child abuse, the visualisation of the psychological struggles of an actress or a stand-up comedian, and the dream-like longing of a boy for the father he never knew. All are subjects of animated films I have designed and directed.

Animation has many unique qualities. One of the most powerful is the visualization of emotions, emotional states, and the personification of inner thoughts. It is for this reason that I feel that animation is the most radical form of cinema, able to literally depict concepts through abstraction, surrealism, and expressionism. Another characteristic of animation is metamorphosis, which John Hubley defines as the "symbolic transformation of energy to describe with sensitivity the complexities of the inner self." Metamorphosis is a marvellous property of animation, yet it rarely makes its way into mainstream productions. Because of its unique properties, animation can be direct and subtle, didactic and amusing all at the same time.

In mainstream media, specifically advertising, animation is often used to diffuse and convey delicate subject matter. Just imagine if that delicacy and directness were to address subjects such as hunger, health problems, overpopulation, war, sexuality and sexual relations, race relations, religion, disease and politics.

Through my New York-based animation company John Canemaker Productions, which was established in 1981, I have specialised in designing and directing films on sensitive topics, such as child abuse,

A sleeping child is sexually attacked in *Break the Silence—Kids Against Child Abuse*

children and cancer, teen suicide, fear of nuclear war, AIDS, and the sources of imagination and creativity. Many of these topics were developed into films which were then produced for programmes seen on United States' broadcast and cable television outlets, such as CBS with *Break the Silence - Kids Against Child Abuse*, which won a 1995 Peabody Award, HBO and *You Don't Have to Die*, a documentary with animation sequences that won an Academy Award as Best Documentary Short, and PBS with *The Creative Spirit*, among others.

In developing animation for the dissemination of information about serious subject matters, I have found that there is a different creative process involved than when dealing with the standard sound cartoon. Following is a brief summary of the three main aspects involved in making serious subjects accessible through animation:

RESEARCH
This is the initial and long process needed to find simple and strong, yet appealing imagery for use in the film. Generally, this process begins with delving into photos, drawings by children, fine art and written information about the chosen subject matter. It is necessary to totally immerse oneself in the data and selective imagery about the topic in order to jump-start the imagination.

An animated portrait of a father who physically abuses his children

CONCEPTS
This second process is a period of exploration in making "inspirational" or concept drawings. Ideas, based on the research, should be allowed to flow without self-censorship. One guiding rule to keep in mind however, is that the ideas for moving graphics should be far from a live-action solution to a problem. In other words, strive to use animation for the unique medium that it is and not be confined to the traditional modes of representation. For example, in the film *Break the Silence - Kids Against Child Abuse*, a physically abusive father was portrayed as an octopus with eight belts and buckles swinging wildly as he chased two tiny children.

STYLE
I often use a child-like or naive art style to diffuse potentially frightening subjects, as well as appeal to youngsters. This serves to

A mother abandons her infant child

help them identify with the drawings as something they themselves might create. In selecting the animation style, I suggest that local animation companies around the world, especially when creating didactic or informational films, explore and use the native designs of that particular region (or the target audience's region) instead of attempting to copy the American studio "cel look." The excellent principles of animation motion and personality, codified by the Walt Disney Studios in the 1930's (i.e. stretch and squash, etc.), are applicable to any and all graphic designs. Use of these important principles in cooperation with all of the techniques available to animation, such as puppetry, cutouts, sand, pinscreen, computers, as well as paper drawings and so on, yields visually rich results and will be more easily accepted by the intended audience.

Keeping these principles in mind, over the past several years I have done a considerable amount of work using children's artwork in my films, and as mentioned above, I animate with artwork drawn in what is considered a naive or child-like style. In order to create the artwork in this style, I begin by trying to put myself on the same psychological level as a child. I strive to present artwork that doesn't look terribly formidable and is not overwhelming. Instead, I create very gentle and accessible animation.

In a similar fashion, I feel it would be quite interesting if the animators who work with UNICEF in regional and field offices could incorporate the indigenous art of the regions in which they work into that area's animation product. I believe this would be a great way to incorporate an interest from the people that UNICEF and similar organisations are trying to communicate with, by showing them that this is their artwork and therefore it is very much a part of their lives. Even the smaller regions within a country must have local artists who are well-known to the people or who at least represent the style or the type of design or artistic philosophy of that region.

The shadowy hand of an abuser

In continuing this process, it might also be very useful to bring these local artists into the actual animation production process. The Walt Disney Company in Hollywood utilises what they call "inspirational sketch artists" who don't really have much to do with the "Disney style" of animation, but instead are artists who are very strong in their own graphic representation. These concept sketch artists present ideas, later adapted into the Disney animation style and feed the whole creative process.

The real strength of the use of animation to communicate difficult subjects is that even the most didactic of films can be used as a springboard for further discussion. In fact, many teachers find animation to be a wonderful supplement to their regular educational materials. Keep in mind that alternative animation films are not meant to be the last word. Rather, the films should be used as a catalyst to encourage discussion of sensitive subjects such as sexuality, AIDS and abuse.

Real social change is most successful when it begins on a grassroots level, and this applies to animation for education as well. It is extremely important that everyone involved in the use of animation as a tool for developmental change works on a local level within their specific regions to achieve a genuine communication. We must involve the people whom the problems and plights conveyed are directly affecting. That is, involve the culture and work from within to communicate these important messages.

A lonely child waits in vain for his/her parents

John Canemaker is an award-winning animator and has produced a number of specials on serious subjects for both broadcast and cable television. He heads the animation programme at New York University.

The Global Network of Animators

Michel Ocelot

The International Animated Film Association (ASIFA) was formed thirty years ago, when people around the world who loved animation decided to get together to talk, forge links, and cooperate in developing their very special art. Since then, the links have grown stronger and the organisation has continued to expand.

ASIFA is an independent organisation, unaffiliated with any government, political party, business entity or sponsor. In spite of its lack of subsidisation, ASIFA has been able to continue working to promote the interests of the animation community. ASIFA plans and stages international festivals and assists filmmakers in planning international festival tours. It also produces newsletters and other publications, including a magazine published in the organisation's three official languages, English, French and Russian. Its singular authority and representative nature have, among other things, allowed people to cross over supposedly unbreachable borders. In effect, ASIFA is an international network of friendships with representatives in over 60 countries.

L'Homme Oui Plantait Des Arbes by Frédérich Bach

As a result of this network, a global link exists between animators in both developed and developing countries to whom ASIFA can lend a hand when they need help.

Animators in several countries have benefited from and in turn greatly enriched ASIFA's work. For example, in China, members have received support for animation festivals as well as for the worldwide dissemination of their work. ASIFA has helped animators in Iran, Cuba, and Mongolia to exhibit their work, organising national and international tours, and in some cases actually helping members to find work. ASIFA offers animators from developing countries an opportunity to maintain a presence in the international arena and be a meaningful part of a larger community of artists.

ASIFA provides a number of facilities to its members, including access to the organisation's film archives, an active worldwide network of children's workshops, and an annually updated job databank and school list. The job databank, located in Prague, provides production studios in developed countries with information about animators in developing countries. Animators who want to be included in the databank fill out a simple questionnaire. Large studios can then access the databank to locate which animators they may want to employ or subcontract for work. The school list provides information to aspiring animators from developing countries about opportunities to study with some of the world's top animators, such as Jiri Barta and Michael Pavlatova in Prague, Paul Driessen in Kassel, Nazarov, Norstein, Khitruk and Khrzhanovsky in Moscow, Jules Engel in Los Angeles, and Chris Hinton and Joyce Borenstein in Montreal.

The partnership between ASIFA and

UNICEF — a fairly new one — is growing stronger as new initiatives and projects are developed. UNICEF and ASIFA are organising a worldwide storyboard competition for ASIFA's 1,500 members, focusing on children's rights and development issues, with the winning entries going into production under UNICEF's banner. ASIFA will publicise the competition in its regional, national and international newsletters, administer and judge the competition, as well as serve in a consultative capacity in UNICEF's production of the selected storyboards. Relationships and contacts have also been established between several of UNICEF's National Committees and ASIFA members in their respective countries to make use of animation in promoting UNICEF messages. One idea for future collaboration is to develop an open forum to promote UNICEF messages amongst ASIFA scriptwriters.

The animation techniques used by ASIFA provide a much different, alternative style of animation to the mainstream methods widely recognised throughout the world. To explain ASIFA's unique methods, it is necessary to first define animation styles. In general, animation styles can be divided into two types. First, there is the classic cartoon, which has a lengthy preparatory phase, including extensive research and analysis. At each stage of creation and production a myriad of teams is performing many compartmentalised tasks. Classic cartoons are also generally the result of an all-important, all-encompassing organisational framework and high costs, and are produced by large industry leaders like Walt Disney. Because of the limited access to this form of animation, it is not hard to imagine that there is another way of doing things.

There is. It's called "handmade" animation. More of a craft than an industrial product, handmade animation is neither better nor worse than the classic cartoon, and like the latter, it has its virtues and its faults. One unique quality of handmade animation is that it can be done with a variety of media: cutouts, pencil drawings on paper, modelling clay, sand, puppets . . . the list goes on. There are a number of benefits in utilising this animation style as well, notably its low cost and the lack of restrictions on where and how it can be done. Because of its flexibility and adaptability, handmade animation can be done practically anywhere with a few very basic tools.

Short films or "shorts" created using this style can be done relatively cheaply by a handful of people if they are willing to wear several hats. I have found that working in small groups can often yield greater rewards. During my rare forays into the larger corporate animation industry, I sometimes detected a strain of dullness among my colleagues, as many workers were simply waiting for "A" to tell them what to do and for "B" to finish the job. In contrast, in the world of handmade animation, I see craftspeople who are creating the work they want to create in a clear and expressive way. The independent animator knows how to size up a problem, adjust his or her sights, and produce something new. I have often been astonished by the solutions independent animators devise as they create better and faster ways to arrive at the end result.

The idea of the craftsperson as artist, who does his or her work eagerly, intelligently and enjoyably, lies at the heart of handmade animation, and it shows in the results. There is considerable merit in using simple means, for when you combine a congenial technique with a clear and cogent message, you have a successful work of art.

Animation made by a small group of people can not only convey the humanity of the film's creators more clearly, but as a result, it has the capacity to produce deeper feelings from the audience. This can be seen in Yuri Norstein's *Tale of Tales*, which was hailed by one international critic as "the best

Since the Second Animation for Development Workshop and Summit, ASIFA President Michel Ocelot has secured the presence of UNICEF prizes at four ASIFA international film festivals—Annecy, Kiev, Ottawa and Zagreb. The prize is awarded to the animated project which best deals with children and children's rights issues.

Crac by Frédérich Bach

Tale of Tales by Yuri Norstein.

animated film of all time and of all countries." *Tale of Tales* was not created by a huge, elaborately structured team, but rather by three people — the Russian author, his wife and a cameraman, cleverly utilising cutout paper.

Independent filmmaker Frédérich Bach does all of his own animation with coloured pencils. His film, *The Man Who Planted Trees,* which won an Oscar among other prestigious prizes, was so powerful that it launched a public and private movement of tree planting around the world. Another of Bach 's films, *Crac*, is a perfect example of the importance of simplicity, honesty and freedom from intimidation coming through in a work of art. In this film, Bach told the story he wanted to tell, in which life passes by and moves onward, against a portrait of Canada, the land he lives in and loves. Bach had expected that because the film was filled with a number of specific details, nobody but people from his home town would appreciate it and that it would have little impact outside the area. However, the basic truth in *Crac* touched people all over the world, and wherever it was shown it was understood instantly by critics, juries (it won every possible prize, including an Oscar), and by the public.

I saw *Crac* in a Paris cinema. At the end of the short screening, the audience, which had come to see the live-action feature which followed, broke into spontaneous applause. I had never seen anything like it. Some years later when I happened to meet the filmmaker, I told him I had seen his film at the Pagode in Paris, and that a captivated audience had given it an ovation. "I know," Bach replied. "The projectionist wrote and told me."

Michel Ocelot is the President of the Association Internationale du Film d'Animation (the International Animated Film Association). ASIFA extends an open invitation to all animators from developing countries to join the Job Databank free of charge. For Databank Questionnaires and information, contact Jiri Kubicek, Strekovska 1342, 18299 Praha 8, Czech Republic, Fax/Phone: (42) 2-858-3203.

Creating Early Childhood Development Materials: A Holistic Management Approach

Cassie Landers & Michael Sporn

Introduction

In many developing countries, early child development programmes reach only a small percentage of those children and families who most need services. Moreover, many early childhood development projects, though innovative, have not been sustainable and have failed to move beyond the pilot stage. To try to overcome limited availability of quality services and respond to increased demand, UNICEF identified a media-based approach as a key to providing information on early childhood development to large numbers of parents and caregivers.

The goal of this media-based initiative is to enhance early child development outcomes by supporting parents and families in their role as primary caregivers. Its specific objective was the design of a four-part animated / live action child development video series and supportive print materials, in order to provide parents and other caregivers with the essential knowledge, strategies, and resources for ensuring children's optimal development during the first six years of life.

The series was designed for national television broadcast. This, together with its availability in videocassette format, encourages its use in a wide variety of group settings, including community-based parent discussion groups, early child development programmes, training courses for professionals and para-professionals, and health care centres. The supporting materials complement ongoing initiatives and can be easily integrated into existing programmes that provide care and education to children and their families.

The initiative has been developed in collaboration with UNICEF New York, UNICEF Jordan and selected countries in the Middle East. Following the initial developmental phase, the materials will be distributed to other countries within the Middle East for local adaptation and subsequently shared with countries in other regions.

This chapter reviews materials developed for this initiative and includes an overview of the animation process. The role and function of the UNICEF Programme Officer in managing and implementing the development of country-specific materials, as well as the implementation of the initiative, are also highlighted.

Designing Materials: Video and Print

In the past, design strategies were limited and were characterised by a number of deficiencies. For example, materials were either developed anew, making little or no effort to use existing resources and materials, or existing materials were used, based on the assumption that little or no modifications were necessary.

In this initiative, an attempt was made to overcome the limitations inherent in these approaches by developing a set of core materials which represented the fundamental messages and universal principles characterising the pattern of a child's early development. These core materials were complemented by a series of protocols, frameworks, and guidebooks designed to stimulate the production of country-specific and culturally relevant materials.

Utilising these guidebooks, users are guided through the planning, design, production, implementation and evaluation of four videos and accompanying materials. A brief discussion of these materials is presented in the following section.

Animated Video Series

In an effort to capture a core body of child development information from birth through the first six years of life, the orderly sequence of developmental change is described through animation. The animated video series consists of four 10-minute videos and accompanying facilitators' and parents' guidebooks. The animation has been designed for use in combination with country-specific live action or to stand alone as an animated series.

Throughout the series, several children illustrate the age-specific progression of skills in language, social, emotional, physical, and motor development. Practical suggestions for what parents can do to support and enhance development are portrayed through simple interactions between children and their caregivers. The titles of the four-part animated child development series are: *Off to a Good Start: The First Year of Life*, *A Time Of Adventure: One and Two Year-Olds*, *Pathways To Learning: Three and Four Year-Olds*, and *Ready For School: Five and Six Year-Olds.* The following section reviews the sequences of tasks involved in creating an animated film and highlights the particular design issues challenging this initiative.

Understanding the Animation Process

Once animation has been chosen as the medium best suited to convey an idea or set of messages, a particular style must be selected from the range of available techniques. Knowledge of the strengths and weaknesses of each technique must be carefully considered and matched against overall project objectives and financial resources. Following the identification of an animation studio with the expertise and capacity to generate the selected style, discussions proceed to issues of budget, contract, and production schedule.

From concept development to completed film, the creation of cel animation follows a well-established sequence of activities. The flow of pre-production, production, and post-production tasks is outlined in the three charts on the following pages. This basic pattern is followed by many animation studios and has been designed for efficiency and cost effectiveness. However, more complex initiatives requiring a more artistic response will deviate from this standard process.

As indicated in the chart, the project director or "client" is responsible for providing feedback and approval at various stages of the process. The client's clear understanding of their role and function defines a partnership that blends the client's goals with the artistic and communication skills of the animation studio. Translating the idea or concept into a clearly conceptualised, visually effective, and culturally appropriate animated film depends on the quality of this collaboration.

The fundamental assumption of this initiative — to create a series of child development films for use in a wide range of countries served by UNICEF — challenged the standard animation process. It was evident from the start of the project that the scripts contained a great deal of information which needed to be conveyed in a short amount of time. This heavy emphasis on content had to be balanced against the need to create an entertaining, visually active film that encouraged viewer behavioural change and didn't overload them with information. Moreover, from a structural point of view, the films required a format that could be used for multiple purposes — as a stand alone series or as segments wrapped around live action sequences.

Since the films were designed for worldwide distribution, a style and tone that considered various cultures and economic levels, as well as individual literacy skills and visual sophistication, had to be achieved. The fundamental challenge was to convey basic child development information through a visual representation schema in a language that acknowledged and respected the vastly different and unbalanced environments which nurture young children.

During pre-production activities, these challenges were reflected in a series of discussions between the artist and the scriptwriter. The scriptwriter would prepare a first draft while the artist would draw a rough storyboard. The script would then be revised to accommodate the artist's feedback, and the storyboard artist would redefine and finalise the drawings. The final storyboard reflected these many discussions concerning style, tone, movement quality, conceptual clarity, and accuracy of the child's behaviours and caregiver interactions at various stages of development. To find a proper film length, an "animatic" was assembled by filming the storyboard drawings and extending them to correspond to the length of the narration sequences.

The design challenges also necessitated several changes in the standard sequence of production activities. Although the soundtrack was narrated in the traditional fashion, the characters, voices, particularly the children's, were recorded in a documentary-like style as they performed activities which mimicked the action in the storyboard. Recording the children's spontaneous and natural commentary outside of a traditional studio setting prevented cartoon-like sounding voices and enabled the narrator to stand apart from the real voices.

To keep the images exciting and conceptually meaningful, it was decided to draw upon artist Henri Matisse's Moroccan art. This painted, illustration-based style enabled the development of realistic images. It also gave us the ability to design our cast without giving them a distinct race or ethnicity and they appeared neither Eastern nor Western, white nor black. These realistic characters, capable of conveying a certain depth and sensitivity, were placed in a variety of abstract backgrounds. The abstract nature of the backgrounds diminished attention to place and time.

To execute this style, the usual animation method of painting flat, solid colours was not appropriate. Rather, animation drawings were done in pencil on paper. Once the movement of the characters was approved in the pencil test stage, the paper drawings were coloured with markers. The markers were then reworked with paint thinner to eliminate the intensity of each colour. These marked, paper drawings were cut out and pasted in registered positions to the acetate sheets (cels). Figure 1 on page 36 illustrates the "ink and paint" stage of this particular animation process. Since each film consisted of approximately 7,500 drawings, it was a time consuming process.

The backgrounds were created using similar techniques. Using an analogous process enabled the characters and backgrounds to blend together, appearing as though they came from the same universe. These background techniques differ from more traditional animated films, in which cartoon characters have dense black outlines and their bright, flat colours separate them from watercolour or gauche backgrounds. Figure 2 illustrates one of the backgrounds created using this technique. As portrayed in Figure 3, the painted cels are placed on top of the background and are checked against the exposure sheets prior to filming.

Adapting and adjusting the traditional cel animation process in this fashion resulted in a unique series of films with dense visuals and a complicated soundtrack. Once the films were complete, responsibility of the project returns to the director, whose task it is to manage the production of complementary live action sequences and print materials, as well as the development of distribution, implementation, and evaluation strategies. The following section reviews some of the materials designed to facilitate these activities.

Animated/Live Action Series

The animated series has also been designed for use in combination with country-specific live action so as to enable multiple uses and applications. While the goal of the animation segments is to provide basic core knowledge, the purpose of the live action segments is to build on the information portrayed in the animation by capturing the strengths, patterns, and practices that enhance child development

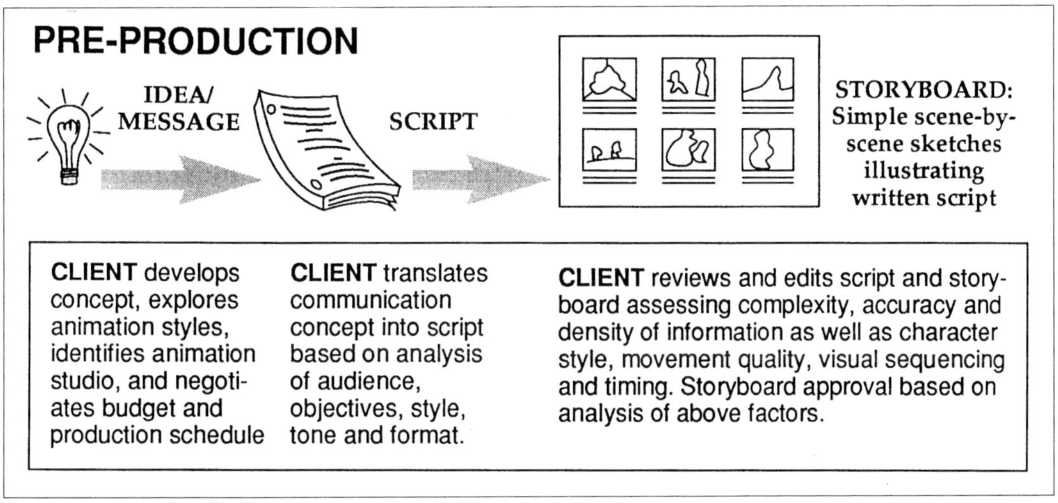

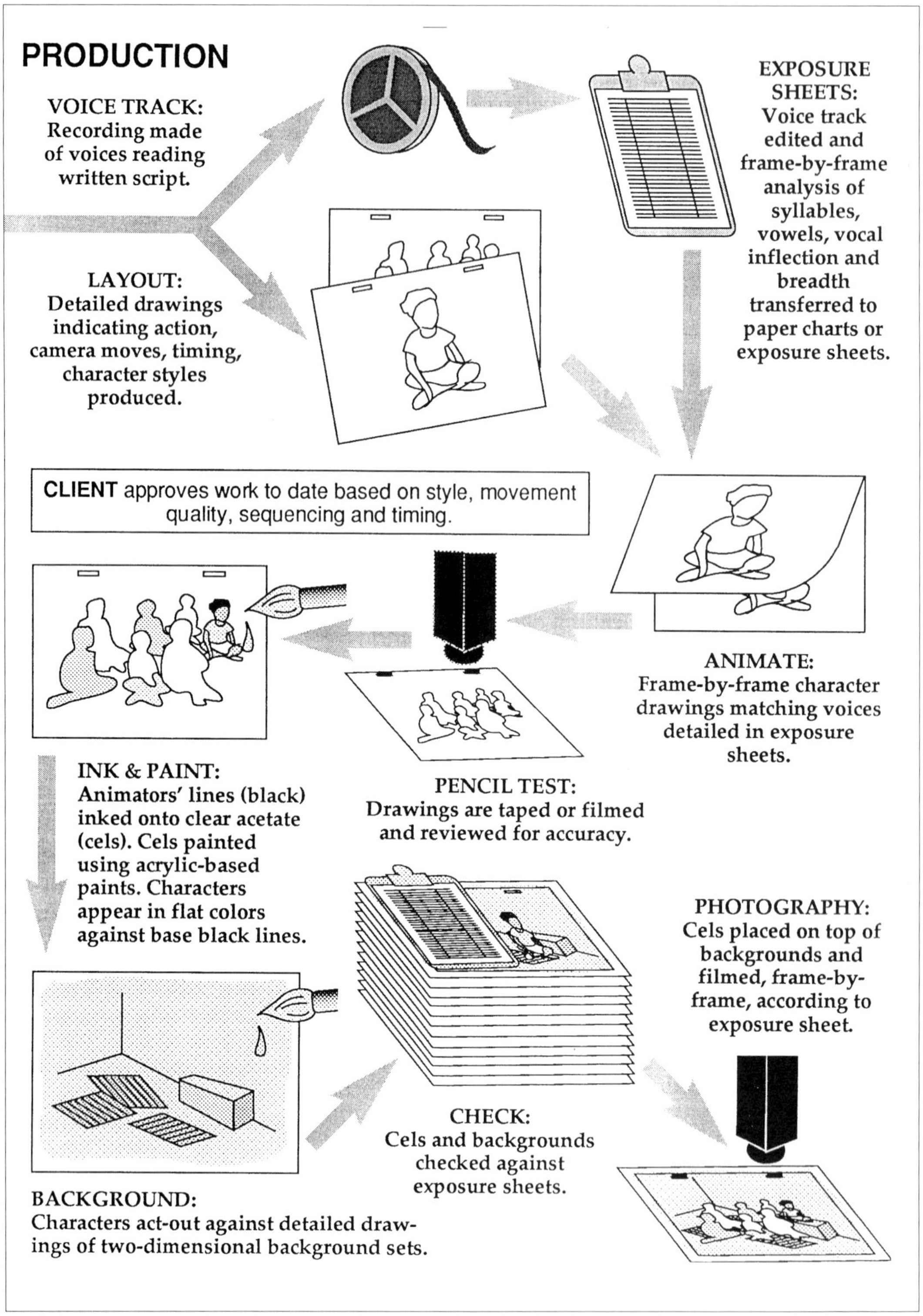

within a particular cultural environment. For each film in the series, a *Production Guidebook* directs the development of a 30-minute video, consisting of approximately eight to ten minutes of animation integrated within twenty minutes of live action. The live action portrays a child's development in common settings and environments, thus illustrating existing positive and culturally-appropriate child care patterns and practices. This approach recognises that behaviour change is more likely to occur through identification with positive role models rather than a critical portrayal of negative practices. Practical suggestions for what parents can do to enhance development and create effective home learning environments are clearly specified.

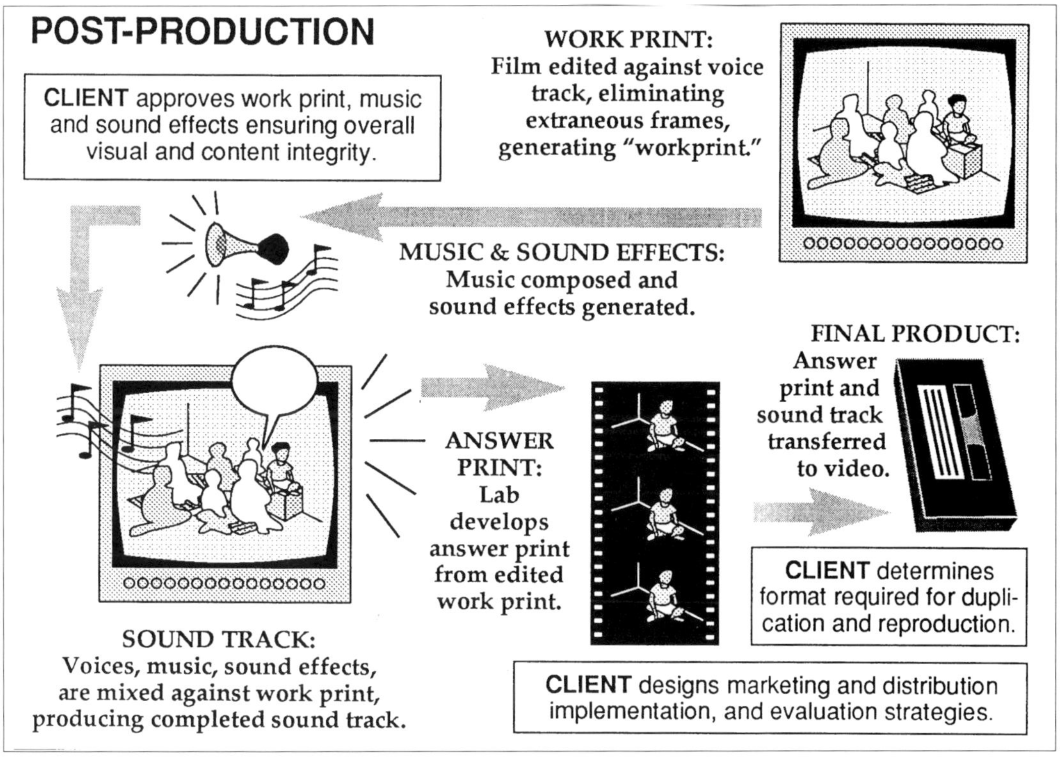

Supportive Print Material

Each video in the series is accompanied by supportive print material, including a *Facilitators' Resource Guide*, as well as parent materials. A set of prototype guides and parents' materials designed for specific country-level adaptation have been developed in an effort to facilitate in-country production activities.

The purpose of the *Facilitators' Resource Guide* is to help health care workers, teachers, early childhood specialists, and community workers to convey the information contained within the video and generate viewer discussions. Facilitators are trained to use the videos in a series of ordered segments with periodic pauses to discuss various aspects of the presentation.

Following the structure of the video, the information contained in the guide is presented in four sections including *Growing and Caring, Moving and Speaking, Thinking and Playing,* and *Feeling and Interacting*. For each section, the main ideas presented in the video are highlighted. Each main idea is followed by a description of the types of viewer behaviour that facilitators should observe as they watch the video. Space is provided for facilitators to make notes about other important behaviours to watch for, and additional questions to think about. In this way, the guide allows facilitators to address specific issues and concerns relevant to a particular group of caregivers.

The parent materials, designed for parents and other caregivers, consist of a set of supplementary materials that highlight the critical information contained within each of the videos. The content is portrayed clearly and simply through illustrations which reinforce programme content and objectives, and suggest materials for use in home-based activities. A set of books based on the animated series is also available for parents and facilitators.

Project Management Guidebooks and Frameworks

A set of guidebooks has been prepared to support UNICEF Programme Officers in managing the wide range of country level production, implementation, and evaluation activities required throughout this initiative. These include: *Message Development Framework; Live Action Production Guidebooks; Community Implementation Framework; Facilitators' Training Guidebook* and *Evaluation Guidebook.*

The *Message Development Framework* includes a three-phase strategy for defining the style and content of the country-specific live action components and supportive print materials. The three phases include background, design, and formative analysis. The background phase reviews issues related to programme objectives, audience, and style. The design phase reviews a set of sequential steps in designing the integration of the animation components within a series of live action segments. The formative analysis phase includes procedures to review content quality and quantity before proceeding to production.

For each video in the series, a *Prototype Production Guidebook* has been prepared to assist countries in the development of the live action segments. Designed as a workbook to enable country-specific adaptation, the *Production Guidebook* contains suggested live action narration, illustrative storyboards, and an alternative shot list indicating additional ways to portray the information. In addition, the guidebooks provide project managers with a synthesised review of the series of steps involved in pre-production, production, and post-production activities.

The *Community Implementation Framework* provides a set of guidelines for managing the design and implementation of the community-based activities including site selection, training of facilitators, and participant selection. This booklet is complemented by a *Facilitators' Training Guidebook*, which outlines a training course for facilitators in how to use the materials in small group discussion sessions. The *Evaluation Guidebook* is a self-instruction guide to all aspects of programme evaluation activities. The guidebook includes sampling protocols, survey instruments, focus group guides, formative evaluation techniques, and outcome instruments. Programme monitoring and data collection strategies are also included.

Organisation and Management

The child development initiative has been designed and managed through the joint collaboration of UNICEF offices. UNICEF New York is responsible for technical coordination, including the design and production of the animated core components, as well as the prototype materials and guidelines designed to stimulate, structure, and operationalize country activities. UNICEF Jordan is responsible for overall inter-country coordination and management and functions as a liaison between New York and the country offices. It is also responsible for translating and distributing project materials and organising technical assistance workshops as required.

The UNICEF Programme Officer at country level is accountable for the overall project design and administration. As illustrated in the table on the facing page, the country-specific tasks are structured according to a five-phase sequence of activities including concept development, design, production, implementation, and evaluation. Under the supervision of the UNICEF Programme Officer, these tasks are carried out through the efforts of a country team comprised of representatives from paediatrics, nutrition, psychology, early education, curriculum development and training, video production and television fields. Ministries of Health, Education, Social Welfare, and the non-governmental organisation community should play a role in advising and supporting the proposed initiative.

The country team is organised into several smaller working groups with responsibility for carrying out the activities in each of the five phases. One working group is responsible for reviewing and refining the concepts contained in the prototype materials and identifying ways in which culture supports, illustrates, and elaborates on these issues. Members of this working group will also be responsible for generating a framework for the live action sequences.

The concept and live action design frameworks are submitted to a second working group to develop, pre-test, and refine the storyboards and script. Responsibilities of this group also include filming, editing, script refinement, and integration of animated core components. The *Production Guidebook* provides guidelines to facilitate these production activities. Members of the country team with expertise in curriculum development are responsible for developing the *Facilitators' Guidebook* and parent materials to

Enhancing ECD: A Video-Based Parent Education Strategy

Project Phases and Activities

PHASE I: CONCEPT DEVELOPMENT
- Review ECD Resource Guide
- Identify country-specific risks, developmental issues and concerns
- Review and critique the animated component
- Develop overall concept framework
- Develop visual representation strategy

PHASE II: DESIGN
- Identify video production technical assistance team
- Prepare storyboards
- Pre-test and revise script and storyboards
- Design *Facilitators' Guidebook*
- Design *Parents' Guidebook* / supportive materials
- Pre-test and revise guidebooks / supportive materials
- Design broadcast implementation strategy
- Design national ECD parent survey
- Design community-based training, implementation and evaluation strategy
- Design community-based evaluation strategy

PHASE III: PRODUCTION
- Video production audio-track
- Integrate country-specific video and animated core
- Editing
- Video reproduction
- Guidebooks and supportive materials production

PHASE IV: IMPLEMENTATION
- National television broadcast
- Distribute videos / guidebooks to community settings
- Implement community-based activities

PHASE V: EVALUATION
- Implement a national ECD survey
- Evaluate viewers' response to televsion broadcast
- Monitor and evaluate community-based activities

accompany each of the videos.

Representatives from national television are selected to design and implement the media-based activities. *Utilising the Community Implementation Framework*, a strategy for reaching parents and other caregivers through existing services and institutions is designed by individuals with expertise in community development. This working group also coordinates materials distribution, community facilitator training, and monitoring and evaluation activities.

Challenges and Opportunities

The early childhood development initiative is based on the premise that a child's early development can be enhanced by providing parents and caregivers access to relevant and practical information. A second assumption is the acceptance that a core body of knowledge transcends all boundaries of race or culture. This knowledge defines not only the sequential pattern of child development throughout the early years, but also a set of critical caregiver responses and behaviours needed to support and enrich optimal growth. At the same time, the many varied environments, which at times either nurture or impede the child's growth, contribute to

Figure 1

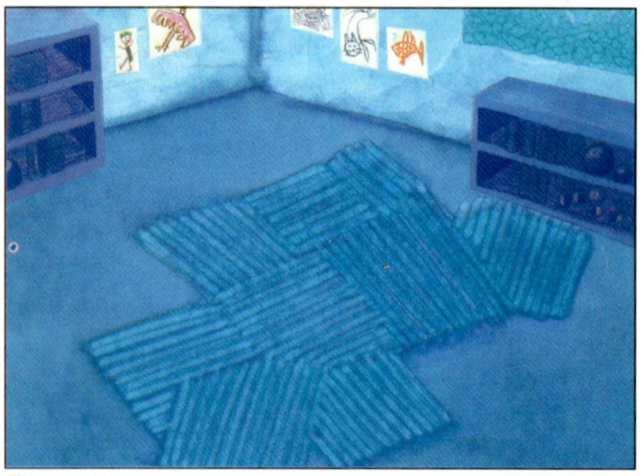

Figure 2

Figure 3

the heterogeneous behaviours that characterise the world's family of children. Variations in the patterns and practices of child care as they interact with the processes of child development must be understood and respected. This blending of universal themes with cultural specific aspects of child care and development guided the design of the initiative.

The development of a set of core child development materials is the first step in this communications process. The remaining challenge is to evaluate the degree to which these goals have been achieved, and to assess the country capacity to achieve broad-scale media coverage complemented by community-based programme activities.

The basic question requiring systematic analysis is how well the visual style created through animation communicates messages across cultural and ethnic boundaries. A related question compares and contrasts the effectiveness of the animated films as a series which stand alone against their usefulness as segments wrapped around a live action series. In essence, can animation be used successfully in a variety of formats for a range of applications?

Another set of issues concerns the cost-effectiveness of a multi-country effort in which materials are designed to be used across countries and regions. In other words, what has been the success and failure of the three-level management approach where UNICEF Headquarters, Regional Offices and selected country offices are asked to join forces in the collaborative development of materials and strategies? In order to ensure programme sustainability and quality control, what can and should be the role of each in the marketing and distribution of the materials?

Perhaps the most important set of questions asks to what extent the framework and design strategy that blends a core body of information with culturally specific information can be utilised in supporting other UNICEF health, education, and nutrition programmes. If the initiative, as it adapts and changes in response to implementation challenges and constraints, is monitored and evaluated closely, the insights gained can only enhance our ability to design and manage more effective communication initiatives.

Cassie Landers is a consultant for UNICEF's Education Division and is a specialist in childhood development.

Michael Sporn is an award-winning animator who most recently produced four animated films on early childhood development for UNICEF.

Formative Research in the Meena Communication Initiative

Mira Aghi

Preface

The tradition of formative research in South Asia goes back to the Satellite Instructional Television Experiment (SITE) conducted during the mid-seventies in India by the Indian Space Research Organisation and Doordarshan, the national television broadcasting authority. The formative research process introduced in this experiment soon gained legitimacy in India. Professionals recognised its ability to make programmes responsive to the needs of the viewers, thereby ensuring their ultimate success. Viewers valued their involvement in the production process.

As a pioneer of this approach in South Asia, I discovered that formative research was not a fixed methodology, but rather had the potential to evolve to suit the demands of each situation. It had to be continually adapted as I was thrown the successive challenges of designing and producing communication strategies and materials aimed at behavioural change. I realised that a communications initiative had to start from the people and not from the professional, and that it was necessary first to learn from peoples' experiences and then to build on that knowledge to design a product for their consumption.

This realisation was further strengthened when I was faced with the challenge of making films on the issues of the girl child in South Asia as part of the Meena Communication Initiative. The films that have been produced bear testimony to the value of the formative research methodology, which has evolved to such a degree that the ownership of the films rests totally with the people. This chapter attempts to show how formative research helped to make this happen.

What is Formative Research?

Formative research is used to design and produce a particular material or communications strategy aimed at bringing about behavioural change. Formative

Hanna-Barbera's Bill Hanna (right) and Buzz Potamkin review educational booklets published for the *Meena* series which was produced by UNICEF in collaboration with Hanna-Barbera Cartoons

research refers to all of the investigations pursued before a final product is produced. The finished product could be tangible material, such as a book, poster, radio or television programme, or it could be a communications strategy used to achieve a particular objective. The aim of this approach is to make the product as relevant and responsive as possible to the audience. Formative research has the unique ability to weed out all unnecessary and irrelevant elements from the product, thereby rendering it highly 'saleable' and acceptable.

Unlike summative research, the success of formative research does not depend on the number of respondents the research process involves. If one gets all the guidance that one needs by talking with only a few people in small focus groups or in one-on-one interviews, then the objective is achieved. The key issue is not the number of respondents, but the depth into which the research goes. The researcher-subject interaction is like the clinical probing of the psychologist with his patient. Rather than talking or advising, the focus is on an active listening, creating an atmosphere of ease and trust after posing the right question to the subject. The ingenuity of the researcher is in asking questions in a manner which will elicit a genuine and informative response. If the question does not produce the required response, it indicates the limitations of the researcher, not the respondent. There is no right or wrong answer in this kind of research — the total data is qualitative and descriptive. The skill of the researcher lies in the interpretation of this data.

The respondents selected for formative research are determined by the subject matter under investigation. The researcher has to look at all those segments of the population to whom the strategy or material needs to relate. Some issues concern specific groups, while others are relevant to the whole population. In this case, the researcher will go to each strata of society to undertake the research.

Meena Communication Initiative

Meena is the heroine of an animated film series developed by UNICEF and its partners in South Asia. This film series is part of a set of communications materials which aim to promote the status of the girl child in South Asia. The stories about Meena are full of adventure and fun, but at their heart lie the real-life problems faced by female children.

The governments of South Asia named the 1990s as the *Decade of the Girl Child*, aiming to confront the extreme discrimination against girls in the region. In order to bring about a transformation in the lives of girls, a radical and creative mass communication initiative was necessary to reach every level and sector of society. The Meena Communication Initiative is a response to this need. It was developed in a unique collaborative venture between Bangladesh, India, Pakistan and Nepal, where the deprivations of the girl child are most acute. Each episode of the animated film series was researched and developed within South Asia. The animated films were then produced jointly by Ram Mohan's Lightbox studios in Bombay and Hanna-Barbera's subsidiary in Manila. An extensive formative research programme was designed to ensure that the final films were presented from the perspective of South Asian audiences and reflected their own needs and interests.

Formative Research in the Meena Series

Before initiating the research programme for the *Meena* series, the underlying assumptions were clarified. Its objective was to highlight the problems faced by girls in South Asia. These issues had to be raised, discussed and dealt with in such a manner that society at large could recognise and could understand that they hindered the development of girls. These problems needed to be solved in order to help young girls to achieve their potential. Just as the problems had to be recognised by the girl, her family and community, so the solutions had to be acceptable to them as well.

These solutions had to fit into the lives of the people. The people must feel that they are their solutions. Therefore, in the Meena Initiative, people were made partners in the creation of the films from the beginning. Initially, the problems were discussed with people to determine how they understood, saw, felt and experienced them. People's perceptions, suggestions and anecdotes were used to evolve a storyline, which was discussed and modified repeatedly, until they were satisfied with the portrayal of the problem and with the solution suggested. Only then were the films produced. As the *Meena* films were intended to relate to the countries and cultures of South Asia, each group needed to participate in this creative process.

Research in the Meena Communication Initiative sought to find out how the stories could play a significant role in bringing about desirable changes in the attitudes and behaviour of people towards the girl child. The extensive research programme was designed to ensure that the films and other materials would be accepted by people throughout Bangladesh, India, Pakistan and Nepal. Through rigorous research, the project sought to identify characters, background settings and storylines which struck a common chord of cultural identity across such a widely heterogeneous population. Meena herself had to be kept close to reality and not become a "supergirl." It was vital that every girl in the region would be able to relate to her and the problems she confronts. Her actions had to be credible.

Formative research was also used to ascertain that each episode of the *Meena* series maintained the delicate balance between "education" and "entertainment" — between weighty social issues and entertaining stories that appeal to both children and adults. Particular care was taken to prevent the film episodes from becoming overloaded with messages or, alternatively, to ensure that a serious issue was not treated flippantly.

The formative research on the *Meena* series examined people's understanding of each issue or message, the appropriateness of the storyline and characters, and the acceptability of the solution to the cultural milieu. This was done through exhaustive sessions with people to reveal their attitudes and values regarding specific topics. These sessions also determined whether or not the issues raised were of real concern to the girls and their families and whether they considered the solutions as viable. The *Meena* series seeks to promote behaviour which is universally acceptable and does not alienate any particular community or section of society, so it was also important that the behaviour proposed did not discriminate against anyone. For example, the cause of girls should not be promoted at the cost of boys.

Formative research in animated film production was used at a number of stages in the development process. The role and objectives of the research were defined by the stage of development.

Research on concepts

Initially, UNICEF would identify an issue which they perceived to be a priority problem in South Asia, such as early marriage or unequal distribution of food. The researcher's task is then to validate this concept with the people — to establish whether or not they really do consider this to be a problem. The researcher introduces the topic to the group discussion and probes their attitudes, beliefs and values in their understanding of the issue. People discuss different dimensions of the problem and are stimulated to suggest solutions.

Research on draft storylines

Findings from concept research are used to develop initial storyline drafts for the films. These are reviewed by technical experts within and outside UNICEF. These storylines, which blend educational and social concepts with adventure and humour, are then taken back to the people to establish the storyline's entertainment value, comprehension and credibility. The researcher either reads the story or plays a pre-recorded version on audiocassette. Respondents are urged to suggest changes and improvements to any aspect. Several storylines are eliminated in the process. With feedback from research groups, stories are modified by the scriptwriters and then returned to the field once again for further testing. This refining process continues until the respondents, researchers and scriptwriters are satisfied with the story.

Research on storyboard animatic videos

The final storyline is produced as a series of still colour images from the storyboard filmed on video with a single narrator. This is recorded in the four main languages of the region. The respondents view this "animatic" video and discuss how the issue is treated. They are invited to step into the shoes of different characters in various situations and see if they can guide the film. The concept and storyline are again validated in this process. At this stage, they can also respond to the visual representation of characters and events. Attention is given to visual details, such as the characters' expression and dress and the houses and scenery, to ensure their acceptability across the region. For example, the artist's impression of Meena's grandmother was strongly rejected because she looked too cruel. Only when the feedback from research in four countries has been synthesised and agreement reached on all aspects of the film, is it taken forward for production.

Once the animated film is complete, it is once again tested for its impact and the ways in which it can be exploited to maximise its effectiveness. Lessons learned from this post-test are used in the

The above two versions of the character Meena were used in research which led to the creation of the final character below.

development of subsequent episodes. Other elements of the Meena communication package, such as posters, stories for radio and audio cassettes, and comic books are pre-tested in the same way with their target audience. Through this participative research process, the *Meena* films and other materials are not made for people, but rather made by people themselves.

Formative Research Process: How We Do It

Plans are made to conduct simultaneous research in the four countries involved. Broad guidelines and strategies are set up in order to pursue a uniform approach. Research tools are designed to fit each stage of the film's development. These tools for data collection are themselves pre-tested. Research sites in different parts of the countries are mapped out.

Qualitative research methods — focus group discussions, focused small group interviews, in-depth one-on-one interviews and observation techniques — are used for data collection. Group discussions have five to seven respondents, while interviews are conducted with a maximum of three people. Animatic videos are screened with groups of ten to twelve people. On average, each film episode is pre-tested through 200 focus groups and fifty in-depth interviews spread across the four countries.

Schedules and guides for data collection include:

- A structured questionnaire to collect general information about the selected field site and people;
- An observation schedule to study the attention and reactions of the group through non-verbal expressions, while watching the animatic video or listening to the storyline;
- A semi-structured questionnaire for group discussions on the stories and videos and for gauging their attitudes and beliefs;
- A semi-structured questionnaire for focus group interviews to study, in detail, the responses of the audience to various aspects of the material.

Open-ended questions are used to elicit the audience's spontaneous impressions and responses. Leading questions are avoided. At each research site, local contacts are tapped prior to field work to help make arrangements for equipment, transport and local participation.

At each pre-test site, people are requested to form small groups. They are introduced to the research team and the purpose of their visit is explained. The researcher stresses the importance of the respondents' role in helping to make a film that will educate and entertain people in many countries, and that it is now in the respondents' hands to see that whatever goes into the storyline / films is appropriate, relevant, realistic and acceptable.

The story / film is then presented to the people without interruption. Following the presentation, the researcher initiates a discussion. While the group is taken through the questionnaire, two research assistants take notes. Feedback from respondents is then analysed at a debriefing session held by the researchers and assistants after returning from the field. A typical research session lasts about two hours and often includes a series of shorter sessions at the same site with different groups of people.

Issues that are controversial or sensitive in a particular socio-cultural setting are tackled through private interviews or small group interviews. In Pakistan, for example, no mixed groups would acknowledge that there was any discrimination in the distribution of food between boys and girls. Girls were then gathered separately in small groups. When asked what instructions their mothers gave them if their brothers were coming home late for a meal, they acknowledged that they were told to save the best pieces of meat for their brothers. Similarly, other issues such as son preference, gender determination of the child and HIV / AIDS were investigated in select groups. In looking at these sensitive issues, it is often more revealing to discuss them in the third person. For example, if a mother is asked directly whether she gives more food to her son than to her daughter, she may well deny it and become defensive. However, if the researcher asks whether there are any families nearby who might behave in this way, a more open response will be elicited.

EXAMPLES OF QUESTIONS IN FORMATIVE RESEARCH

Below is a sample of the general questions usually asked to clarify the concept at the start of the research process. The issue under discussion could be anything from dowry to dehydration to discrimination. It is important to note that the researcher cannot pre-determine the order in which the questions will be asked. This will depend on how the interview progresses.

- What is meant by [topic]?
- What do people mean when they talk about this?
- Have you heard your friends / neighbours talk about it?
- In what context do they talk about it?
- Does this problem really exist?
- How can this problem be explained in your view?
- Do you think other people also think similarly?
- What do men think about it? Women? Girls? Boys? Old people? Young people?
- Can you tell me any story or anecdote you might have heard about it?
- How can a film deal with this issue? What would you like to show?

Once the concept has been validated and the draft storyline developed, pre-testing involves questions on:

- Comprehension and credibility of content
- Appropriateness to country and culture
- Acceptability of characters and roles
- Educational messages / issues
- Practicability of solution
- Agreement with overall philosophy of the series.

At this stage, the most significant questions are geared towards establishing the contextual reality. Examples of such questions include:

- Is this what really happens?
- Do you believe this story / film?
- Will other people / your friends believe this?
- Will this help in any way to change people's attitudes and behaviour?
- What do you think is not right / not acceptable / not real?
- How can the story / film be improved?
- Suggest alternative stories

The animatic / storyboard videos are pretested mainly to establish:

- Comprehension of the story
- Acceptability and credibility of the story and visuals
- Appeal and entertainment value of the story

The Research Team

Simultaneous research was conducted in the four countries participating in the Meena Communication Initiative. A Research Director trained research groups in each country and coordinated and supervised their work to ensure consistency of method and analysis. The same personnel were retained throughout the entire research programme. They were also given special orientation on the philosophy guiding the formative / participative research process — that the respondents must be respected and their opinions valued, irrespective of their background, appearance and educational status. Whatever people say is important and must be analysed and interpreted carefully.

People and Place

The *Meena* film series is intended for the general public, so research was conducted with a wide range of socio-economic groups. In each country, at various stages of development, films were pre-tested in urban slums, peri-urban and rural areas. Depending on the issue to be discussed, the groups would be homogenous or heterogeneous. The groups were stratified by age, sex, educational level, socio-economic class, geographical location and religion. Specific groups, such as teachers, social workers or doctors, were involved as required.

Since the Meena Initiative is directed both at children and adults, it was necessary to involve both in the research. Children, and particularly girls, were included to reflect on the development of the girl heroine, Meena. It was important to ensure that girls were able to relate to Meena and her experiences. Adults were needed to advise on the issues and credibility of each film and to indicate its potential to change adult behaviour towards girls. Meena is intended to be an advocate for the girl child in society as a whole, so the widest possible range of participants in the research process were involved to ensure the project's broad acceptability. The members of the groups were tailored to suit the needs of each topic. For example, in the episode on teasing, *The Bully and the Watermelon*, research was conducted with school boys and girls in mixed and separate groups. Parents and teachers were also interviewed. The issue of dowry was taken to a complete cross section of socio-economic classes, and groups were held with mothers and mothers-in-law,

© UNICEF, Animation by Ram Mohan Lightbox

The chicken thief being chased by Meena and the other villagers

Above & Below: © UNICEF
Animation by Ram Mohan Lightbox

From left to right, initial sketches of the chicken thief, Meena and her brother Raju used during formative research. All three sketches © UNICEF

fathers and fathers-in-law, marriage-age sons and daughters, and younger children. Village headmen and social workers were also interviewed.

Reactions and Response

The pre-testing of the *Meena* film series was a wonderful experience. Each session was a chapter in learning how the concept of Meena works and what potential it has. The process has provided rich feedback, central to developing and refining each episode. It has enriched our understanding of the fundamental nature and potential of qualitative, participative research.

The project has been welcomed by people everywhere. They were willing to cooperate and eager to participate in the creation of the stories. Their response was usually eager and excited. If people were at all inhibited when discussing a sensitive issue, the matter was taken up later in more private groups. If resistance or disharmony ever developed in the focus group discussions, it was enough to wait and watch while people themselves resolved the issue. Significantly, people remarked repeatedly that this was the first time that professionals had approached them for suggestions. Usually, they were at the receiving end of advice.

Respondents have expressed positive opinions about the Meena Initiative, saying they believe these stories will have a good impact in changing attitudes towards the girl child. Meena herself has usually emerged as someone who commands appreciation — admired for her courage, presence of mind and concern for others. Girls relate to her. They want to be Meena. They identify with the problem-solving skills that Meena shows. Adults admire her, support her and seek to strengthen her role. The affluent and the poor speak of Meena with similar affection and find her stories acceptable. Research has demonstrated that Meena can be used with varied audiences across the region. Children can recognise their own experiences and so relate to the stories, while adults take a look at their own attitudes, and work out what they need to do to change them.

Research has shown that animation in the *Meena* films is a powerful and appealing medium for communicating ideas. It teaches while it fascinates and delights. As a result of the research process, animation is being used to address the sensitive gender issues in an open but non-threatening way, thus working to enlighten people without alienating them. Balancing fun and seriousness ensures that the films are not overloaded with messages. Animation engages people with the story and thereby conveys the ideas through the process of identification with the characters and events.

The commonality of responses from different parts of Bangladesh, India, Pakistan and Nepal and has shown that the *Meena* films do indeed have a universal appeal and potential for use with people of all ages and classes across the region. It is the formative research process which has ensured that people identify closely with the issues raised in the films and look upon Meena herself as one of their own.

Mira Aghi was the primary researcher on the Meena Communication Initiative and the African Girl Child Initiative.

Example of Research on a Meena Film

EPISODE: *Dividing the Mango*
ISSUE: DISCRIMINATION IN FOOD AND WORKLOAD LIFE
SKILLS: CRITICAL THINKING; PROBLEM SOLVING

SYNOPSIS OF STORY:
One day, Meena brings home a juicy mango. She is very disappointed when her mother gives a larger share to her little brother, Raju. "That's the way it is," says her grandmother, claiming boys need more food than girls. Meena's father points out that Meena is also a growing child and that she works very hard. When Raju dismisses girls' work as easy, Meena playfully suggests that she and her brother change places the next day. Meena has a delightful day playing with her pet parrot, while keeping watch on the cow. Raju, on the other hand, is exhausted by all Meena's household tasks. "I've never been so hungry!" Raju complains at supper that night. Through Meena's game, her family realises that food should be shared equally.

SUMMARY OF KEY FINDINGS:

- Discrimination in food distribution is based on both quantity and quality. In poorer areas of South Asia girls were deprived on both accounts, whereas in Pakistan girls received less 'quality' food (which people perceive as meat, fish, eggs and dairy products). Both concepts therefore needed to be incorporated in the film.
- The reasons for giving less food to girls focused on the issue of work. It was felt that boys 'needed' more food because their work is outdoors and perceived to be harder than girls' domestic work. The storyline therefore emphasised both the energy required for girls' work and the fact that boys and girls, as growing children, have an equal need of good food.
- While recognition needed to be given to the burden of girls' work, it was not credible to show boys' work as effortless. Therefore, Meena faces some problems when the cow runs away.
- In the original storyline, the grandmother was felt to look and behave too sternly, without showing any affection for Meena. Her role was softened.
- The grandmother originally stated that it was a "tradition" that girls get less food than boys. Since the word "tradition" was often interpreted as something desirable, it was replaced by the expression: "That's the way it is."
- The mother was originally depicted as unsympathetic to Meena. This was revised to show the mother as amused by Meena's antics and a willing participant in her game.
- Discrimination against daughters in food distribution was a highly sensitive issue, its existence often denied. The Meena story provided a non-threatening way to initiate discussion, accessing people's real experiences.

Each research group had six or seven members. Groups were selected from a range of socio-economic backgrounds.

Animated Film and Communication for Empowerment

Rachel Carnegie

Introduction

Since the first workshop on animated film for development in Prague in 1990, UNICEF has launched a number of creative and innovative communication projects. The objectives and scope of these projects vary widely, but they are based on a central premise — that animation is a uniquely powerful and appealing medium for communicating ideas.

The wonder of a moving image fascinates people. It has a particular capacity to delight and teach. It entertains — a magic carpet provides a thrilling world trip, a cat and mouse fool each other with outrageous tricks, a little girl sends her parrot to school to study. It educates — the process of dehydration through diarrhoea is explained, the stages of a child's development is illustrated, the forms of discrimination against girls are exposed. Through animation an idea can be expressed in its simplest form, without any unnecessary detail. The pre-production planning process allows for very close collaboration between the writer, subject specialist and animator so that every word and visual image is precise and intentional. For those involved in development communication, animation offers an exceptional opportunity.

This chapter seeks to highlight the main lessons learned through the Meena Communication Initiative and is drawn from my own experiences in South Asia. I hope that these ideas can be generalised to explore the ways in which UNICEF and its partners can maximise the potential of the animated film and the family of animated characters it has created. In particular, I propose that animated film be launched as the flagship for a fleet of multimedia materials which build on the popularity of the animated characters to reinforce the ideas presented. Through this multi-media perspective, I will also suggest how animated film, which is essentially seen as a medium for mass communication, can also be used at the community level to initiate a process of empowerment education.

Animated Characters as Communication Vehicles

Universal appeal of animation

The Meena Initiative in South Asia exploits the fascination of animation to draw an audience of both children and adults. In the past, communication on the needs and rights of children has often been directed at adults. Yet children and young people also have a right to be informed and can often acquire the skills and motivation to become effective agents of change. They are also a valuable group to mobilise — in many developing countries, nearly half the population is under the age of sixteen.

Research has shown that animation appeals across generations. If the production is well researched and the issues convincingly presented, adults find it a credible and entertaining source of ideas. In the animated characters, children can recognise their own experiences and find their own voices. As a little girl in a Dhaka slum claimed, "I want to be like Meena. I want to go to school too." Through Meena's story, this little girl had been able to articulate her own aspirations and identify her rights. Likewise, parents become engaged with the issues and characters and review their own attitudes towards their daughters. With access to a universal audience, animation therefore has a unique potential as a medium of communication.

Advocates for child rights

Many of the animation projects arose in response to a specific regional priority. In South Asia, the 1990s' *Decade of the Girl Child* gave a clear impetus to focus on the urgent problem of discrimination against girls in the region.

Whatever their primary focus, all of the initiatives are underpinned by the vision of the *Convention on the Rights of the Child*, an agreement endorsing children's rights under international law. By popularising the needs and rights of children, society as a whole can grow more conscious of its duties and obligations. The challenge is to make these rights relevant and meaningful to children's lives. The endearing animated characters speak for the rights of children and give them a voice. Meanwhile, through their charm they steal into the hearts and minds of their audience and start to work on them from within.

Child rights concerns often touch upon controversial and sensitive issues buried within a culture. Through animation, the topic can be addressed in an open yet unthreatening way. While remaining honest and direct about the issue, animated film can disarm its audience's usual defences.

This is the case with Meena. She is a delightful, funny, spirited character. The stories revolve around the adventures of Meena, her brother, Raju, and her pet parrot, Mithu. Meena's experiences expose discrimination against girls and women and offer positive insights into how this can be overcome. In the first episode, she longs to go to school, but her parents believe that girls do not need to be educated. So instead, Meena sends her parrot to school to learn in her place. Using the knowledge the parrot brings back to her, Meena manages to catch a chicken thief. Through this adventure, she finally convinces her parents that, like her brother, she too has a right to education.

Meena presents a dynamic role model for girls in the region, as well as a powerful advocate for the girl child's rights. The Meena stories present many positive images of a girl who succeeds against the odds to gain equal treatment and respect. While the underlying messages are serious, the stories are fun and full of fantasy to make the most of the entertainment value of animation. The response of audiences at all levels of society has illustrated the special universal appeal of Meena as a cartoon character and as a symbol for the girl child. Children love her for her humour and playfulness, and adults feel moved by her plight and inspired by her courageous behaviour. The girl child is encouraged to believe that she has the same value as her brother and a right to equal treatment and opportunities. Her parents gain new insights and are encouraged to reconsider their own attitudes and obligations to their daughter.

Promoters of the Decade Goals

In a number of UNICEF's projects, animated film has been used effectively to communicate the messages of the Decade Goals — UNICEF's objectives for the survival and development of women and children. However, the success of these communication initiatives may bring about its own problems.

Once a character has become popular, there may be demands to use it as a vehicle for many other messages. The initiative could literally get pulled in too many directions. It is important that a character or film series doesn't become overloaded with messages and lose its original focus. For example, it was recently suggested that an animated spot featuring Meena should be made for all of UNICEF's survival and development messages that pertain to women and children. There is much debate as to whether the Meena character should only deal with issues specifically concerning the girl child, or whether the scope should be broadened to incorporate other Decade Goals on health, nutrition, water and sanitation. Can animated characters speak for all health and development issues, or will this dilute their impact?

In the case of Meena, the project goal was to establish her as a regional symbol for the girl child. However, once that objective is achieved it may be possible to have her endorse other issues while retaining her primary focus. Hence, Meena now appears on posters promoting Oral Rehydration Therapy (ORT). In the Meena Initiative, guidelines have now been prepared to indicate the ways in which Meena can be used, while still retaining the integrity of her image as a symbol for the girl child.

The guidelines for protecting Meena's image are most important outside UNICEF's context. They came into use when a large non-government organisation (NGO) in Bangladesh, along with thousands of schools, proposed using Meena and Raju as the main characters in an English language course. These lessons were to be recorded for radio using 18-year-old actors to play their parts. The initiative was well-intentioned, but the effect would have been to confuse of Meena's public image. In a more positive example of spontaneous use, paintings of Meena have started to appear on rickshaws around Dhaka, Bangladesh. Obviously it is neither possible nor desirable to maintain rigid control over Meena's image, since it is a sign of success that the characters have become part of the local culture. However, it is still important to guard against losing absolute control and risk damaging the integrity of the image.

When determining how many issues or messages the characters will speak for, it is also vital to consider the balance of entertainment and education. While some of the animated films remain didactic in nature, in others the characters have become popular precisely because they entertain rather than preach. The ratio of 90% entertainment to 10% education is an important one. It is vital that the comedy and storyline are not overwhelmed by too many messages. Research has shown that the most effective and sustained communication occurs when audiences actively engage with the issues, storyline and characters, not when they are the passive recipients of a one-way flow of information.

From Information to Empowerment

The transfer of essential information must be combined with a process of empowerment which allows people to utilise such knowledge effectively. This enables people to examine their lives critically and become aware of their ability to control their own circumstances.

In development communication, this issue of empowerment needs to be reflected both in the research and development of the materials and in their subsequent utilisation within the community. In both instances, the communicator is seeking to promote a critical consciousness in people — to enable them to engage in a process of critical thinking leading to action. For example, in the formative and summative research (before and after production) of the Meena film on unequal food distribution, it was found that parents initially denied discriminating against their daughters. However, after learning Meena's story, the respondents gradually came to acknowledge that they do discriminate, not only in food distribution, but in many other aspects of child rearing. This led to a discussion on what action they could take to resolve this issue.

The Research Process: Giving People a Voice

The importance and value of in-depth formative research has been demonstrated in many of UNICEF's animation projects. The aim of the research is not just to test the comprehension of the message, but also to test the appropriateness of the story treatment to the culture and gauge the acceptability of the characters. Beyond that, it seeks to enter into an authentic dialogue with the respondents to reveal their attitudes and values surrounding an issue.

Formative research can help to make the respondents active participants in developing the concepts and materials. When analysing whether a learning process has been active or passive, a key question to ask is, "Who provided the knowledge?" In an active learning approach, the people evaluate the information according to their own experiences and transform it so that it becomes their own knowledge. While the technical information may derive from the experts, formative research can ensure that the messages are reinterpreted in the idiom of the people.

In aiming to address the rights and needs of children, we need to examine decision-making processes in families and other relationships as well as the dynamics of such communication. The content of communication materials should therefore not only address people's needs, but also the context in which they live and how their environment affects their ability to take action and meet those needs. The storylines in animated films can illustrate these contexts and show how individuals become empowered.

In the *Meena* stories, the characters demonstrate how they cope with life by acquiring psycho-social and cognitive life skills. These skills include critical thinking, problem-solving, decision-making, and psycho-social skills such as communication, negotiation, assertiveness, coping with stress and resisting peer pressure.

Meena is shown acquiring skills in solving problems, resolving conflicts and communicating effectively. As such, she represents a very positive role model for girls' empowerment, emphasizing girls' potential, rather than showing them as victims. For example, when her female cousin is teased by a group of boys, Meena assertively uses the power of group solidarity to confront the bullies.

© UNICEF

Young girls reading stories from the *Meena* series

STRATEGIES FOR EMPOWERMENT: PROMOTING THE DIALOGUE

The way in which communication materials are utilised is crucial in moving towards an empowering learning process rather than a didactic, one-way flow of information. When using the mass media as a vehicle for communication, we can maximise its impact by planning for community-based educational and outreach activities. New strategies include the development of resource books and videos which will enable teachers, facilitators, parents and communities to use the materials for more effective learning. Capacity building and training is also important for partners in the government as well as for NGOs working at community level. In essence, the animated film and other materials can be used through the mass media for advocacy and awareness-raising, and at community level as a tool for promoting dialogue and inter-active learning.

As a term, *empowerment* has lost its force and precision of meaning through over-usage. However, there is general agreement that information alone cannot empower people to take action. The concept of empowerment involves a process of growth and development in the learners, and leads to deliberate efforts by the learners to transform the circumstances of their lives. Such a process of learning encourages a Freirean cycle of critical thinking, action and reflection. This process can produce radical results:

> "Instead of being preached to, [people] become subjects of their own learning as they ask questions, explore the many levels of the problem, make decisions for their own choices, and share the seriousness of the issue with friends and communities."
> Wallerstein and Bernstein, Empowerment Education, *Health Education Quarterly*, Vol.15 1988, p. 385).

By involving individuals in a group process, this model promotes active learning on a cognitive level. But it also fosters active learning on a behavioural level, cultivating assertive communication skills and a sense of personal and social responsibility. This has been the focus of many of the *Child-to-Child* health education projects in different countries. The *Child-to-Child* approach aims to provide children with the knowledge, skills and motivation to take action in their families and communities.

During the next phase of the Meena Initiative, the focus of activities will be on developing materials and providing training and capacity building with partners to enable them to facilitate group processes. The support materials being developed will promote group discussion and *Child-to-Child* approaches. They seek to reinforce a process of empowerment through exploring how the issues raised in the Meena stories relate to the audience's own lives, and what action the group can take to address these concerns.

Programming for Behavioural and Social Development

The elements required for behavioural development programming can be described as the provision of information, motivation, ability of people to act (including the development of life skills), an enabling environment of supportive family, peers, community and services, as well as appropriate policy and legislation. This model suggests a mass media initiative with carefully programmed educational and outreach components to reach and influence all levels and sectors of society. The popularity of animation offers an suitable vehicle for undertaking such ambitious aims. Well- designed and researched animation characters can become recognized household names, embodying a set of ideas across a region and beyond. This is especially so when these animated characters are further popularized through multimedia support materials.

Multimedia and multi-channel

Animation is sometimes criticised as an inappropriate medium for communication in developing countries, since it relies on electronic projection and transmission. Yet, with the revolution in communications technology, access to electronic media in South Asia is dramatically expanding and will continue to do so over the next decade. However, the issue of access to different channels is important and should influence the range of materials which are developed. While animation has a unique fascination and appeal to excite a nation's imagination and create national impact, we must also consider how to reach the young girl who does not attend school in the remotest rural village. To reinforce and extend the outreach and impact of the film series, a multimedia package can be created. National and regional differences in access to channels will influence the emphasis placed on various media.

In the Meena Initiative, the multimedia package being developed includes: storybooks (which also serve as supplementary readers), posters, audiocassettes, a radio series co-produced with the BBC World Service, folk-media, including puppets, songs, masked drama, resource kits and guidelines for group discussion, and child-to-child activities. In addition, individual UNICEF offices have produced documentaries to accompany the animated film episodes, positioning Meena in the context of their own countries.

On an experimental basis, promotional merchandise has also been tested on the market in Bangladesh. At present, the commercial products are aimed at the urban middle class and use cause-related marketing to make them sympathetic to the girl child concerns. Future merchandising will attempt to popularise Meena's image, as well as establish the financial sustainability of the project.

Outreach strategies: working with governments and NGOs

Creating an "enabling environment" for behavioural and social change requires a communication strategy that reaches all levels of society. At one level, advocacy is needed to develop and maintain political and social commitment to the cause. At another level, alliances need to be built with partners in the government and NGO sector to ensure coordinated and sustained action. Finally, at the community level, materials, dissemination channels and communication activities are required to support people's learning and decision making. The following model for the Meena project is an example of this communication strategy.

In the Meena Initiative, UNICEF's advocacy contributed towards placing the issue of the girl child onto the regional agenda and led to the declaration of the South Asian *Decade of the Girl Child* in 1990. Three years later, the first episode of Meena and some promotional materials were presented to the South Asian Heads of State at their summit meeting. At a country level, sustained advocacy with policymakers helps ensure that the girl child concerns remain on the political agenda.

In terms of alliance building, UNICEF's Communication and Information Officers in every country office have built an impressive network of partners with the government, NGOs and the private sector. These partners have been mobilised to incorporate the Meena materials into their own educational and communication activities. As a result, the films and audio versions are being broadcast on national and local TV and radio. The films are being distributed by cinemas as well as government mobile film units, which can reach remote rural areas. The printed materials are used in both formal and non-formal education programmes. For example, ten million copies of the Meena comic book were distributed by the Ministry of Primary Education in Bangladesh. In one Indian state, "Meena Clubs" have been set up in primary schools.

As the project moves into the outreach phase, the diversity and effect of these partner activities will be intensified. A series of impact studies in the different countries will identify the most effective approaches. Capacity building and communication training of partners will form a major element of this phase. A crucial aspect of alliance building has been to involve the government and NGO partners in the design and development of the materials, so that they share in a sense of ownership.

Finally, at community level, the Meena Initiative is using a multi-media, multi-channel approach to try to reach the widest audience. Through its resource materials and training programmes with project partners, it will also promote a more participatory, interactive form of communication, based on the concept of empowerment as described above.

WORKING WITH THE COMMERCIAL SECTOR

The idea of commercial partnerships is, in some ways, unchartered territory. *Meena* was born out of a collaboration between UNICEF and Hanna-Barbera Cartoons. Six *Meena* episodes have currently been produced by Hanna-Barbera through Fil-Cartoons, based in Manila, the Philippines. The Meena Initiative has also co-produced a radio series in Bengali with the BBC World Service.

UNICEF and the entertainment industry can be seen to share many of the same concerns. While UNICEF is involved with the well-being of children, the entertainment industry is looking for issues which will interest children and young people. An obvious example is the topic of adolescent sexuality — a perennial subject in soap operas, and a key area of concern for UNICEF in the prevention of teenage pregnancy and AIDS. Joint programme development could usefully address these important subjects, while sustaining a strong and entertaining storyline.

As UNICEF's animation projects increase in size and popularity, there is a growing imperative to address the need for financial sustainability. Partnership with the commercial sector offers many opportunities for production and distribution, as well as for sponsorship and licensing. Bringing a commercial dimension to these UNICEF communication projects also presents many challenges.

To anticipate some of the issues arising from corporate partnerships, UNICEF commissioned a Global Business Plan for the Meena Initiative. This includes guidelines on international legal provisions for UNICEF's copyright of the character and materials, as well as licensing of the image. It also recommends strategies for negotiating with broadcasters, for regional and global marketing and distribution of the films and other media through different channels, and for merchandising of the image. It is estimated that a consumer market of 300 million exists in South Asia as potential buyers of Meena merchandise. The business plan also confirms that there is an interest in the Meena film series in industrialised countries. The first episode is currently being dubbed into eight European languages for use in children's broadcasting and education for development. There is strong interest in continuing the series beyond the first thirteen episodes to maintain the momentum of the initiative. This will depend upon forging sustainable partnerships with commercial producers and distributors.

Conclusion

The experiences of the Meena Initiative in the use of animated film in development communication provide valuable insights as we pioneer new territory. There is much to be learned from the various dimensions of this project — the process of creative development, the different animation techniques, the process of formative and summative research, the creation of multi-media and multi-channel interventions, and the use of animated film and support materials to promote dialogue and action at all levels of society. These lessons will enable us to maximise the potential of animated film as an educational and entertaining tool for communication for empowerment.

Rachel Carnegie was a consultant to UNICEF from 1991 through 1994 and was responsible for co-ordination and creative direction of the Meena Communication Initiative for the Girl Child in South Asia.

The Adolescent Girl Communication Initiative of Eastern and Southern Africa

Neill McKee

Introduction

In the Eastern and Southern African Region (ESAR), the female child faces gender discrimination which begins at birth and continues throughout her life, affecting her education, access to health care and social services, and workload in the home. She has less opportunities than boys in almost all areas of human endeavour. She is generally regarded as someone who is "just passing through" the home and, consequently, the family invests less in her care and development. At an early age, she learns to play a subservient role in the family.

As a result of these circumstances, she grows up without basic psycho-social skills such as the ability to communicate her feelings, to negotiate, to solve problems and resolve conflicts, and so she enters relationships with the opposite sex as an unequal partner. This inequality leads to many social problems which have tremendous impact on the entire community. One of the most recent and serious manifestations of this situation is the sharp increase in the AIDS pandemic throughout Sub-Saharan Africa.

A radical, creative mass communications initiative is needed to transform the situation of girl children through behavioural development and change. An environment that can sustain this change must be built. Because animation can communicate sensitive issues, animated films have been chosen as the flagship for this important initiative. Addressing the problems of the adolescent girl in a region plagued by AIDS is a tremendous challenge for the medium. Emphasis will also be placed on radio and print materials because of the limited reach of audiovisual media in this part of Africa; a multimedia approach is therefore envisaged.

Status of the Girl Child in ESAR

In ESAR, many countries are experiencing economic decline and complex emergencies, in which women and children are most severely affected. Urgent action is needed to change pervasive discrimination against females. Within ESAR there has been increasing emphasis by governments, non-government organisations (NGOs) and donor agencies to close the gender gap and overcome discrimination against girl children.

However, there are many customs and traditions which affect the development of female children. The difference between boys' and girls' upbringing begins in the very first hour of life, when there is much more value and attention given to the boy. In some countries, the birth of a boy is accompanied by five ululations, whereas a girl is welcomed by only three. Sometimes women are beaten for not giving birth to a boy. When sickness strikes, male children are taken to the hospital immediately, while girls have to wait until the very last moment, which is often too late. Mortality rates are higher among female children.

Stereotyping and role-modelling starts at a very early age. Girls are sometimes referred to in derogatory terms or as someone who doesn't belong. As they grow older, girls must serve male family members, care for younger children, fetch water and firewood, wash clothes and cook. When her mother leaves the household to earn an income, it is the girl who has to take over her role. In this spiral of servitude and work, she is denied childhood.

Parents attach less importance to girls' education than to that of boys. If resources allow for only one child to be sent to school, the parents will generally decide in favour of the boy. Although a preliminary study of seventeen ESAR countries shows a closing of the gender gap to four percent in primary school enrolment, for girls there is a much higher repetition rate throughout the primary years. As a result, the ratio at completion is as low as one girl to ten boys. This disadvantage in educational opportunities also robs the girl of her chance to be a child, as school is one of the few

© UNICEF

Some of the characters in development for the Adolescent Girl Communication Initiative of Eastern and Southern Africa.

places where she can socialise with other children.

This negative socialisation process gives the girl a sense of inferiority, resulting in a negative self-concept. The stereotype is reinforced by the way girls and women are defined in school curricula, textbooks and various media. The overall result is a girl child with a limited perception of her own capabilities and possibilities.

As the girl grows, the disparities in treatment and status are compounded. The problem of "teenage motherhood" is endemic in the ESAR. Thousands of adolescent girls get pregnant every year. They are often not yet ready, physically or psychologically, for motherhood. They are often thrown out of the educational system. These girls are victims of their unequal position in society. They are also in much greater danger of falling ill with numerous diseases — some thirty percent of maternal deaths occur among teenagers.

The situation of adolescent girls becomes even more worrying in the context of AIDS. The pandemic has hit the region harder than any other area of the world. Rape, adolescent pregnancies, and practices such as multiple partner relationships, female genital mutilation, initiation rites, forced marriage and polygamy have all contributed to the rapid spread of HIV.

All of these conditions have an extremely negative impact on the development and empowerment of the female child.

© UNICEF

A focus group discussion during research for the Adolescent Girl Communication Initiative.

She is unable to recognise her own problems and cannot express her needs. With such social and cultural conditioning, girls are denied vital skills like decision-making, problem solving, critical thinking, negotiation, empathy, self-awareness, assertiveness and resistance which could help protect them against HIV / AIDS and many other threats to their well-being. Only when knowledge of health and social issues are combined with these life-skill competencies will girls and women be able to take charge of their own destiny and make a real impact on their own lives.

To bring about a transformation in the situation of the adolescent female, a dynamic, creative and far-reaching communication strategy is required. However, this strategy must have a solid grounding, including extensive audience research into the values and perceptions about the girl child's status and how it can be improved.

A Multimedia Symbol of Empowerment

While it is possible to present the female child as a victim requiring assistance and protection, it is more important to recognise her proactive potential as a leading agent in promoting development. The Adolescent Girl Communication Initiative aims to develop a symbol of an empowered girl who, through creative and exciting stories, will promote solutions to social problems in an appealing, entertaining and provocative way. The object is to develop a character who will become a household name, acting as a powerful symbol and advocate for the empowerment of the girl child.

The visual components of the project include animated films, comic books and posters. In viewing photographs or live-action films, people in multi-ethnic environments have been found to respond to cultural and social cues such as dress, facial features, language and accents, and housing and vegetation, all of which may alienate and distract them. They may be fascinated by what they see, but at the same time miss the main message and conclude that the situations posed are "someone else's problem." However, with proper formative research, a set of characters, backgrounds and stories can be designed in animated film and cartoon formats which strike a common chord across a diverse region.

In the African Girl Child Initiative, the animated film is the medium through which a set of characters and stories come to life, because animated film can capture the attention and imagination of audiences and provide a creative focus. Although access to television is relatively low and urban-based in much of Africa, broadcast statistics do not account for the growing informal channels of film and video distribution in the continent. In many countries, numerous networks exist for the distribution of videos — through NGOs, churches, commercial outlets and other channels. Videos are shown in public places such as restaurants, bars and "video theatres," which are quickly growing in small communities. Film theatres and mobile cinema circuits reach millions of urban people every month.

© UNICEF

At the same time, the strength of radio as a communications medium in the region, combined with the oral cultural tradition in Africa, means that a radio series is required as a strong component of this endeavour. Radio, comparatively speaking, is a flexible and inexpensive medium and the stories can easily be adapted for use in any broadcast language. However, like television, video or film, there is little evidence that radio by itself has a sustained impact on behaviour. While radio can provide information, develop an awareness of issues and motivate people, this is only a first step to behavioural change.

The complexity of factors required for successful behaviour change indicates the need for a multi-media approach, led by a medium which will capture the imagination and attention of a wide cross-section of the public, beginning with opinion setters, educators and dwellers in urban areas. That medium is animation. The episodes must be informative and motivate at the same time. This can be achieved through the use of entertaining stories based on research into values, attitudes and perceptions. They must address the life skills and enabling environment factors which are so often omitted from behaviour programming. Finally, they must be formatted in a package, elements of which can be used for formal and non-formal broadcast and education processes.

Launching the Initiative

In October 1994, the initiative was launched at a regional workshop in Machakos, Kenya, with sixty-five participants including gender specialists, researchers, educational media

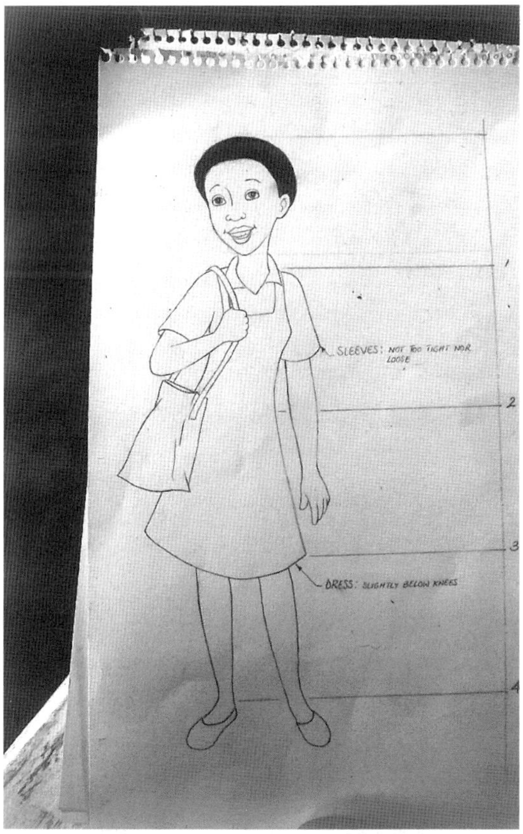

Left & above: Pencil sketches of the leading character

producers and artists from the participating countries in the region. Exercises in gender awareness and behaviour change and role-playing of adolescent problems led to story development. Draft storylines were concept tested and pre-tested on schoolchildren, out-of-school youth and adults. Artists were trained in design elements of both animation and comic books, and began to draw and shape their concepts of an adolescent girl through theme development. Regional characters, backgrounds and draft storyboards were created for further development following the workshop. A core team of artists was identified for more extensive training and involvement in the project.

After the workshop, UNICEF put out an open call throughout the region for story ideas. By the end of 1994, forty concepts had come in, dealing with many of the themes identified in the initial workshop, including HIV / AIDS, sexual abuse, early marriage, teenage pregnancy, education, career choices, female genital mutilation, workload and the issue of preference for sons. This response made it possible to accelerate the progress of the initiative. All stories were subjected to critical analysis and later revised by their authors where necessary.

The top four stories and the best visual concepts were then selected for use in a research training workshop for Eastern Africa held in Jinja, Uganda in January 1995. A workshop for Southern Africa was held in Malawi in February 1995. Workshop participants were given in-depth training on focus group methodology by Dr. Mira Aghi, chief researcher of the Meena Communication Initiative developed in South Asia. During the workshops, the national teams drew up their research plans and returned to their countries to carry out the initial phase of research in mid-May 1995.

At time of writing, a regional research synthesis workshop is planned for early June 1995 at which researchers, writers and artists will bring together the findings on four story concepts, revise the storylines, arrive at character and background features with the widest appeal, and make a decision on the names of the characters to be used in the stories. The writers will then revise their stories to include full dialogue, and artists will finalise the character models and begin producing storyboards. Key drawings will be produced for at least three of the stories for further research in the region. At the end of this process, the story with the most potential for an animated film will be produced in animatic form — key drawings on video with script — and taken to the field for feedback from target audiences. After this imperative research, the final production process can begin.

© UNICEF

A storyline visualised during the workshop held at Machakos.

Going to Scale

Once this first animated piece is complete, the project will be thoroughly evaluated before the second phase of the initiative is launched. In Phase Two a series of episodes will be developed using the media found to be the most successful and useful throughout the region. The weight given to producing more animated film will be determined through such feedback. This phase will also involve further training of regional artists and communication researchers. At the same time, all participating countries will be encouraged to develop and implement action plans for dissemination of the materials through broadcast, government, NGO and commercial channels. Strategic plans will be developed for broadcasting and licensing of the series in the region and around the world. Links with the international entertainment industry are being sought to facilitate this process. An attempt will also be made to establish the initiative as a self-sustaining, non-profit enterprise, through marketing of the communications package and merchandising of the characters/images to finance the activities.

Conclusion

The African Girl Child Initiative is a bold attempt to address the problems of the girl child in Africa. Nothing less than this is needed to change the existing situation. A whole generation of girls is at risk and their survival and development will determine the health and well-being of future generations. Without a radical change in the situation of the adolescent girl, Africa's future looks bleak indeed.

© UNICEF

A role-play of teenage pregnancy.

Themes of the Adolescent Girl Communication Initiative

Core problems

- Preference for sons
- Early marriage
- Teenage pregnancy
- Sexual abuse/harassment
- Female genital mutilation
- HIV/AIDS and STDs
- Workload
- Limited access to education
- "Push out" from school

Related problems

- Poor family life education
- Lack of career options/counselling
- Limited societal expectations
- Exploitation in employment
- Violence and abuse, especially in emergencies
- Lack of economic opportunities
- Low access to health care
- Growing commercial sex roles/sugar daddies
- Substance abuse
- Suicide

Neill McKee is the Senior Programme Communications Officer for UNICEF's Eastern and Southern Africa Regional Office and the author of *Social Mobilization and Social Marketing in Developing Communities*.

Merchandising Programme Management: It All Begins with a Strategy

Glenda Banales

When shopping have you ever noticed how stores with similar product lines will seem very different? Perhaps there are stores that come to mind that are always in stock with just the right items and are visually exciting. Does the average consumer realise the amount of time and resources it takes to plan, analyse, create and execute such a unique shopping experience?

Probably not! But that's good! The highest compliment a consumer can pay a retailer is return visits and referrals. Shopping is an activity that should be an enjoyable, hassle-free, seamless experience. It all begins with a strategy . . .

This chapter is a topside summary of the many aspects of building a merchandise programme. Each aspect is dependent on the other in order to keep to the overall merchandise strategy and deadlines. If each is followed, the end result will reflect consistency, integrity, quality and a high degree of professionalism. The managing of a merchandise programme or product line is essential when working across many different types of product categories and classifications.

A programme is an assortment of merchandise that supports a common theme, property, attraction, cause or event. The assortment usually crosses many categories and classifications and is typically displayed together in order to create a strong visual impact. An assortment within a programme can be as simple as a few items or as complex as mixing a variety of product categories and classifications.

No matter what the size or the objective of creating the programme, the process should always remain consistent. In order to achieve consistency, programme development functions should flow through a time line. Depending on the complexity of the organisation, the time line should always remain flexible and easy to maintain.

When considering whether to combine a group of items or a programme, the following should first be determined:

- What is the programme?
- What are the opportunities within the programme?
- What are the parameters?

In other words, one should understand the full scope of the programme before proceeding.

Once the definition has been established and the scope fully realised, the overall objective of the programme must be determined. Here are a few considerations:

- **Capitalise on external trends or events** - Is there an uprising trend or theme occurring in the marketplace, community, country or the world? If so, what benefit would it have on the proposed programme?
- **Fulfil an experience of need** - Would the proposed programme or products assist the user in creating or experiencing a feeling or mood or meeting a specific need?
- **Create or fulfil a demand** - Is the programme or products line marketing in such a way to communicate a "one and only" or "first to have" need? If so, then a demand will be either created or fulfilled.
- **Focus on existing business drivers** - Is there a character, product or trend that is currently driving the business or a demand? If so, how can it be enhanced or what other opportunities exist?

Once the major objectives are realised, the potential of the programme can be identified. This step should determine the validity and profitability of the programme, as well as whether or not the process should continue.

In order to identify a programme's potential, one must determine if the objective is non-profit or for-profit purposes. The major objective of non-profit business is to inform, enlighten and educate a service, topic or issue that involves the health and welfare of our environment and/or world, whereas the major objective of for-profit business is determined by a financial analysis. Once the analysis is established, the proposed programme is either validated or cancelled. A financial analysis reflects all incurred costs (product development, labour, manufacturing, shipping, delivery, warehousing, royalties, visual set-up and enhancements, etc.) and should also include the topside assortment, duration, topside distribution and marketing support. An analysis should also be done for non-profit programmes — the difference is changing the emphasis from revenue to awareness. Whatever the objective, all costs should always be captured. Once it is established whether the objective is non-profit or for-profit, an overall business plan should be prepared.

Now that a programme's definition, scope, objective and business plan are fully understood and agreed upon, the strategic planning can begin. The strategic plan should always be monitored by a time line. This is a programme manager's most valuable tool.

A time line is much more than a list of dates. It is the programme manager's checklist. If it is truly utilised, it can not only assist in the programme flow, but can also pinpoint potential problems. After the time line is established, the strategic plan can be implemented. This plan outlines and establishes the programme direction, theme and scope. This is particularly important if the strategy must be communicated to several sources.

The merchandise strategy should consist of all key aspects of a programme:

- Duration - delivery, store set-up, promotion, consolidation and termination
- Event / release date
- Promotional support
- Objective
- Target market - demographics
- Theme
- Key stories
- Characters
- Art direction - style, coloration
- Assortment and location distribution
- Visual enhancements

Here is an overall summary of each aspect of the merchandise strategy:

Duration

If a programme is driven by a set promotional or release date, all other dates in the time line are easily calculated. It is just a matter of knowing the timing of each task and then working backwards from the set-up dates and forward for consolidation and termination, always keeping in mind the complexity of your business operation, production lead-time, manufacturer's shipping, warehouse system and distribution. In order to build an accurate time line, all task dates must be taken into consideration.

Event/Release Date

If the programme is driven by a hard date, then this date should be documented and communicated to all those concerned.

Promotional Support

This support usually falls in line with the marketing strategy. Besides building a strong merchandise plan, what other internal efforts are in-process? This could be advertising (print or electronic), guest appearances, parades, sponsorship or signage. Whatever the magnitude of the advertising, make sure the merchandise presentation is consistent with all promotional support. This will substantiate the overall message.

Objective

As stated earlier, an overall objective must be identified in order to give a better understanding of the programme. What is it that must be accomplished or achieved from the effort and expense? The perceived accomplishment or outcome must always be greater than the current status. If it is not, then perhaps the time, money and effort should be spent elsewhere.

Target Market

In order to understand and gain optimum results, a programme's target market must be identified, evaluated and understood:

• Who will want to purchase the product or understand the overall messages of the programme? Does the company have a void or special interest group in mind?

• Towards whom should the promotional message be aimed? At what age, gender, degree of education or social economics?

• Who will assist in achieving the programme's overall objective?

• Where can the target be found? Where do they live, work and play? (This is very important in supporting the promotional effort).

The above questions can be answered in a variety of ways:

- Focus groups
- Polls, questionnaires or surveys
- Consumer, environmental, community, revenue or market known voids.

Theme

A theme is very important to a programme as it will set and maintain its creative direction. Therefore it is critical to know and understand the complete scope of the programme. The challenge is to find the theme or visual statement within the programme that will translate to the target market. Depending on the complexity of the programme, this task could involve many hours of researching and brainstorming.

Understand the programme:

- What are the key elements of the programme? (Break down each element and elaborate on what exactly is happening or who are the important characters.) This is then broken down to determine any underlying meanings or hidden values.
- What are the key scenes? (backgrounds, places, colorations)
- Who are the primary characters? (personalities, costumes, expressions)
- What morals exist? (underlying lesson or meaning)

Key Stories

Once the main theme is determined, if applicable, stories can then be extracted to complete the process. Key stories are obtained by breaking down the primary theme. This should be considered when trying to zero in on multiple target markets. Knowing what these stories are and their magnitude will assist with the creative design direction and scope.

To find these key stories, break down the subject or work into sequences. Then list important scenes, views or morals. This will help the art designer to develop a clearer understanding of the direction. Thus art development time and costs are spent more efficiently. This up-front planning will also assist in keeping to the established time line. (Word of warning: key stories add to the complexity of the programme and therefore should only be applied if further enhancement can be justified).

Characters

In order to communicate to each target, the primary and secondary characters must be identified. Once this is done, the art direction and message can be targeted to the right audience.

Art Direction

Once the business plan theme and merchandise stories are established, the design direction can begin. For best results, this portion of the strategy should be coordinated by the programme manager and art designer. This teamwork is very important in order to maintain character integrity, theme, consistency and overall programme quality. Along with the programme manager, the art designer will select appropriate colorations that will run consistently through the programme. These colours can be found in character costumes, key art elements and backgrounds, as well as forecasting trends.

Once the overall colour palette is determined, it can be broken down by key stories. As the art designer works through the theme, target markets should always be focused. Pinpointing each market will make the creative message better understood, as well as using time and resources more efficiently. Once the creative direction is determined, the programme manager and designer assemble a directional portfolio. This portfolio should contain all aspects of the creative direction, broken down by theme, coloration, target markets and key stories. The portfolio is then distributed to procurement for implementation.

Assortment and Location Distribution

As the designer continues to work on creative art design, the programme manager coordinates the task of obtaining the detailed assortment and distribution plan. Realising that all organisations' expertise varies, it is advised that a planning and distribution team be utilised. The programme manager reviews all programme details (overall business plan, duration, objective, target markets, demographics, theme, etc.) with the planning and distribution team. From this information and by using previous business and programme compatibilities, the assortment can be identified.

Programme compatibles are very important, as they will assist in projecting each item's revenue, thus substantiating the validity of the programme. Therefore the need for consistent, timely reporting is critical throughout the duration of every programme.

By knowing each item's projected revenue, the planner can then determine any potential risk (i.e., art costs, production costs, minimum and maximum quantities, saleability, etc.). Along with the item revenue base, the projected overall revenue will also assist in determining the detailed location item allocation.

As the planner works on the detailed assortment, the distributor keys into the appropriate locations. This is done by comparing existing locations to target markets, preparing a location analysis (projected revenue, location space to sales allocation, displacement factors, promotional efforts, etc.). Once the complete assortment is identified, each item's product development, production and shipping time can be broken down according to the product development process.

The product development process varies from item to item. For instance, from the initial art request submission, a screen printed t-shirt takes considerable less development time than a three-dimensional figurine. This time difference must always be taken into consideration when meeting a hard set-up date. Of course, the given development process time frames can be reduced. But reducing the amount of development time may affect production and shipping costs.

Visual Enhancements

The visual enhancements of a programme can be as simple as themed signage or as complex as refurbishing and theming an entire location. Both approaches can be used together or separately — it all depends on the promotional thrust of the programme (point-of-purchase, single item sales, company supported effort, etc.).

To determine the scope of visual enhancements, the overall marketing effort, which includes all promotional support, must be known This is also very important to the planning and distribution team.

- Where will the promotional activities take place?
- How long will the promotion run?
- What is the theme? What are the key stories?
- How will the promotional support assist in achieving the overall objective?
- Is visual impact important?

Once the answers to these questions are known, then evaluating the need, scope, costs and space for visual enhancement can be determined.

Developing a merchandise programme can be simple or very complex. It usually involves utilising the many talents within and outside the organisation. This effort cannot be achieved in a vacuum, but rather by a team. If the organising, planning and implementing has been done with the highest degree of quality and consistency, the objective will be achieved and the programme will be a success.

Glenda Banales, the Senior Product Manager for Walt Disney Attractions Merchandise, has worked in retail for the past 20 years.

SECTION TWO

Learning to Animate

Training Developing Country Animators: An Introduction

An intrinsic part of all UNICEF projects is a commitment to incorporate the capacity-building and empowerment vital for sustainable development of the programmes it implements. Using animation as a tool for development communication therefore means empowering local artists to use this medium to help children in their communities. To effectively use animation for development, training must serve two purposes: it needs to educate local artists in the technical skills of animation, and to sensitise them to the development issues they need to communicate.

Every society has artistic traditions in drama, music, and art that reinforce its cultural identity, so training artists in animation isn't something that needs to be taught from scratch. Even countries without an established animation industry have artistic communities whose talents can be channeled into this medium. For example, in parts of Africa there are strong traditions in three-dimensional earthwork and claymation. In Indonesia, cutout figures and puppets are popular and could be modified for animation. Providing necessary technical training on animation simply enhances skills that already exist in a community.

As television becomes more and more a global medium, transcending national and even regional boundaries, it is important to ensure that the educational and entertainment messages being broadcast in developing countries are not solely the products of the industrialised world. Locally produced programmes allow people to identify with their own cultural traits and customs and to recieve information that they can relate to in their own country or community contexts. This makes the case for empowering local artists and local media in one area of animation even stronger. Local artists, who are renowned for having a social conscience, have first-hand experience with the issues and problems faced by people in their own communities.

UNICEF and its partners are seeking solutions to the many health, nutritional and social problems that are faced by many communities in the developing world. In many instances, the means to solve these problems are available, but this needs to be reinforced by behavioural and social change. UNICEF can work with local artists so that effective social messages can be translated into action to tackle their community's most pressing problems. Artists can play a crucial role in development communication when their ideas are placed in the context of an overall social development programme.

In this chapter we provide a range of perspectives on animation training. Japanese animator Sayoko Kinoshita looks at animation training through her experiences in Hiroshima, where she specialises in training animators from developing countries. Guy O'Neal, a Barbadian cartoonist, describes his experience as a participant in UNICEF training workshops and his internship at Walt Disney Feature Animation. Jessica Langford, an accomplished animator and teacher at the Edinburgh Film Workshop, describes how children can be brought into the animation process, and provides an overview of animation construction from the storyboard to editing the final product.

UNICEF, its counterparts and the governments with which it works, help children survive and develop. The animation industry has the communication techniques to communicate these messages in an entertaining way, and local artists can adapt them into culturally appropriate forms. Training artists from developing countries in the skills of animation and instilling in them an awareness of development issues will ensure that animation's value as an important tool for social communication increases and becomes part of the sustainable development process.

The Edinburgh Animation Workshop

Jessica Langford

Since 1981, the Edinburgh Animation Workshop has helped people of all ages and abilities make animated films. Set up under an educational charitable trust, the Workshop provides 16mm animation production facilities to independent animators and production training for young people, community groups and people with special needs.

The following extracts are from an animation production book I wrote called *Nothing is Impossible.* The book is intended to be an inspiring guide for people who have not made animation films before and would like to have a go. The most important thing is to have ideas, imagination, enthusiasm and a lot of patience!

Introduction

Animation is one of the simplest, most creative and economic ways of making a film. It provides an ideal introduction to filmmaking for individuals working at home, or young people in schools and community groups. The main advantage of animation is that a minimum of equipment is needed, and this is usually available through a local resource centre.

The Edinburgh Animation Workshop encourages the inclusion of animation production in school curricula. Producing an animated film as a school project involves many processes and skills that make it an ideal educational medium. The whole class plans the story line together and then works in small groups of five. This allows each child to be involved with all the decision-making and creative processes, and to contribute individual ideas and skills to the group.

In the classroom, the theme for the animated piece can be directly linked to a curriculum subject. For example, a complex geometry theory animated with match sticks and plasticine monsters will never be forgotten. Animation can also be used as a focus for children to discuss issues and develop awareness, such as making a film about environmental pollution or conservation. Fantasy ideas can be developed directly from the children's experience — a recent visit to a gallery or a poem or piece of music that they wrote. The most important thing about the theme of the film is that it should provide an opportunity for children to express their ideas.

The Storyboard

The storyboard is a visual script which sets out the main scenes in the film. It gives basic information about action, camera, position, length of shot and sound. It is essential to make a storyboard, so that you have a clear idea of what you want to say and how you want to say it. A storyboard is also essential for continuity, as, in a group, different people may be working on different sequences of the same film. The storyboard process teaches us to edit and structure our ideas, as well as to develop skills in the visual narrative. We learn to look at how films are constructed — the use of varied camera shots and visual effects.

Planning the storyboard

To create a simple storyboard, divide an A4 sheet of paper into four or six boxes. Each box illustrates a different scene. Information about the soundtrack and camera movements is written below the image.

- Break the film down into scenes which logically express the story
- Decide how camera angles and movements can be used to enhance emotional impact of story
- Decide the length of each shot — the pacing and timing of an animated film is crucial, especially if it is humourous
- Use visual clues and continuity — small details in artwork can give clues to time, moods and atmosphere of characters and locale
- Plan effective use of sound in support of, or in contrast to, the image on the screen

Creative Artwork

Animation films can be made from almost anything! You do not need expensive art materials. Imaginative films can be made

Teaching the skill of filming cutouts.

with autumn leaves, salt, sand, feathers and other objects. There are many different techniques and materials that can be used to create the animation, such as plasticine, cutouts, drawings, puppets, and many more.

It is important that the characters don't just look good, but can be used technically — i.e., the character's limbs can be animated a fraction of a centimetre, stay in the same position while they're filmed, and then be moved again. At school, children of different ages and abilities will be able to use some materials and techniques more easily than others. Here is an example of how cutouts could be utilised by young animators.

Cutouts

Cutouts are a good technique to start with, especially for young children, as exciting effects can be achieved simply and in a comparatively short period of time. Materials which can be used for cutouts include: thin white cards, scissors, clear adhesive tape, needles and cotton, crayons, ink, felt-tip pens, fabrics and "blu-tack" or some sort of malleable adhesive. Thin card works better than paper as paper characters curl up from the heat of the lights when you are filming, distorting the character and creating shadows.

The first step in creating a cutout is to design the character. Decide which limbs you need to move and what they have to do in the film. These limbs are then drawn and cut out separately and jointed invisibly with a needle and thread, cotton and masking tape. If, for example, you want your character to walk to the right, turn around, face forwards, and walk back again, you would need to make three different figures, each one facing in a different direction. For facial expressions, the character would need a series of detachable heads, each one with a different expression.

The creation of cutouts for animation can be summarised as follows:

1. Design character
2. Create separate moving limbs
3. Arrange limbs, decide pivot points of joint and tape cotton firmly underneath
4. Put needle through pivot point at base of joint
5. Pull thread firmly so that limb is tight against body — it should move freely but not be too loose
6. Tape cotton to underside of neck and cut off surplus — the joint should be invisible.

One of the main problems with cutouts is that there is no exact record of where the figure has moved from, so the artwork must be animated very carefully. If possible, stick any still parts of the figure to the background with blu-tack so that you do have some control.

Equipment

Animators working in studios use animation rostrums for filming their artwork, unless they are using 3D animation. A rostrum is a special table that can be moved precisely to minute calibrations in any direction. The camera is mounted on a fixed column and can also be moved very precisely up and down. This is used for zooming in or out of scenes. An animation rostrum is a very expensive piece of equipment. Fortunately, a simple rostrum can be improvised and set up at home or school.

MAKING YOUR OWN ROSTRUM

If you are planning to do a lot of animation in the classroom, it may be worth your while to make your own rostrum. This takes up

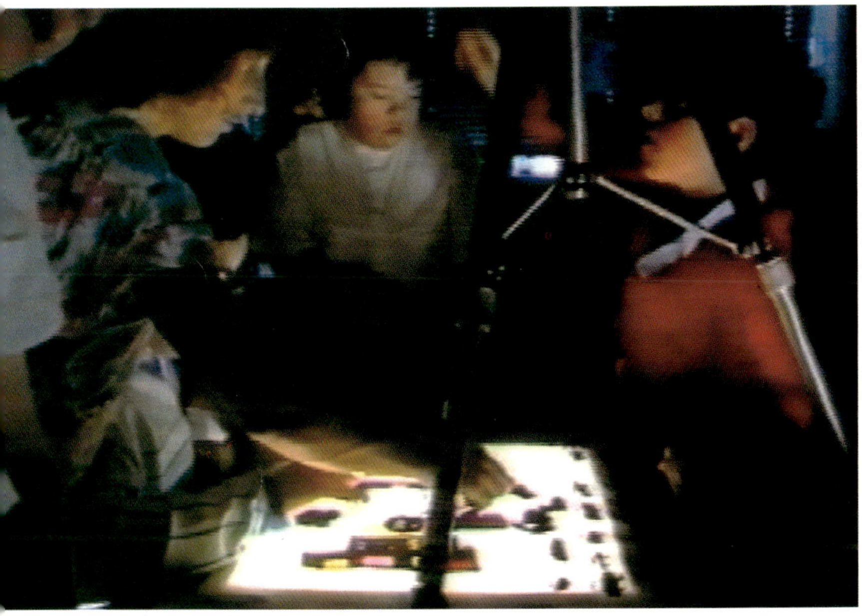

Filming the cutouts as they are manipulated in movement.

© *Nothing's Impossible*, Edinburgh Film Workshop Trust

less space than a tripod and is less clumsy to use. It can be easily set up in a bedroom, garden shed, or in a classroom. It is very important that the camera is firmly fixed and does not shake when you are filming. The camera can be fixed at the minimum focal length above the artwork, usually between three and five feet. The strength of the lights can vary — 150 watts may be enough. It's important that both lights are the same and that the artwork area is evenly lit.

The set up for animation can be quite simple, on film or video. The important factor is that the film or video camera can take one or two frames at a time. The following equipment is necessary:

1. A camera — usually Super 8 or 16mm — with a single-frame facility
2. A good tripod
3. 2 lights with stands
4. A strong table
5. A projector

SETTING UP EQUIPMENT FOR FILMING CUTOUTS, DRAWINGS AND FLAT ARTWORK

Set the tripod on the table and tape it so that it doesn't wobble and can't be jogged. Place the lights on either side of the table, so that the light is distributed as evenly as possible. Fix the camera on the tripod and turn it so that it faces directly downwards. The size of the artwork area on the table may vary, but 40cm by 50cm is a convenient size for children to work with. Stick the background for the scene down firmly with tape or glue so it doesn't move. Make sure the artwork is turned the right way up to the camera and that all hands and shadows are out of the way when you film two frames!

Production and Post-Production

MOVEMENT AND TIMING

Whatever the animation artwork or technique, there is one very simple rule to remember — 1 second of film equals 24 frames. The animator must work to this timing, so if you want a character to move from point "A" to point "B" in one second, 24 frames must be filmed. Fortunately, you can film two frames per movement. If you film more than two frames for each movement, the animation will not be smooth, resulting in pixilation. It will depend on the age and ability of the children how well they can calculate the different timings and movements. It is important that the young ones are not intimidated by the mathematics involved.

EDITING

Once filming is finished and the film has returned from the lab, it may be necessary to edit out a few mistakes and put scenes in the right order. To edit the film you will need the following equipment: a viewer and rewinder, tape splicer, white gloves and white wax pencil.

Project the film several times, so that any mistakes can be clearly seen. Wind the film slowly through the viewer, marking the frames to be cut with the wax pencil and edit the film together with the splicer. Precisely cut the film scene by scene. By physically editing the film, the children will understand how it is technically constructed. Throughout the post-production stages they will become aware of the many processes and skills behind the production of a film.

Sound recording

Sound is an extremely important yet often overlooked aspect of an animated film. Ideas for the dialogue, sound effects and music should be planned during the storyboard development. During filming it is important to animate a character long enough so that it can "speak" the dialogue. This means "Hello, how are you?" needs at least two seconds, so that the characters head or lips should have been animated for 48 frames. Some animators record the soundtrack first, then make a note of each frame and animate to it. When working with children or people without professional film experience, it is easier to record the sound after the picture.

Creating the soundtrack is a very exciting process. Children can experiment with their voices, creating character's accents and strange sound effects, or improvising with musical instruments to create a piece of music for their film. If no sound recording equipment is available at the school, the children can still get a lot of pleasure and satisfaction from showing their film to an audience and creating a live soundtrack as their film is projected.

The Screening

Once young animators have finished their work, the screening is one of their greatest rewards. Not only does the screening provide an opportunity for the children to present their work to parents and friends, but it also gives them a chance to organise an event themselves — making invitations, contacting the local press, organising the evening, looking after the audience and providing refreshments.

Whether you are showing your film to friends at home or to a large audience, it is always a special occasion. Make sure that the projector works properly — that the lens is clean, the image fits well on the screen and the "blackout" is as good as possible. If you are showing the film to a group, you may like to show some other animation films which can be ordered from distributors.

At school the screening may be for the class, the whole school or parents and friends. The children should feel proud of themselves for having worked through the whole animation process and solved the different problems that arose. There is also great satisfaction in the realisation that each of them have contributed their individual ideas and skills to produce something together. Before the screening, especially if it is for parents and friends, it is good for the children to put up an exhibition of their artwork and maybe some photos of their film in production.

Animation provides an opportunity for people of all ages and abilities to produce their own films. It is an ideal educational medium, involving imagination, storytelling, design, artwork, drama, music and technical skills. It enables people to have a very direct involvement with the production. This means that the film is a vehicle for not only expressing the groups' ideas or message, but a very personal reflection of their culture. The stories, artwork and music provide a unique insight into people's lives and values. Most importantly, animation enables people who are often only 'receivers' of television to participate.

Jessica Langford established the Edinburgh Film Workshop Trust's Animation Workshop in 1981 and is currently the president of the ASIFA Workshop Committee.

The Disney Internship Experience

Guy O'Neal

My fascination with and love for the world of animation began when I was very young. Like many kids, I used to love watching Disney and Hanna-Barbera cartoons on television. My favourite character was Woody Woodpecker. However, despite this early interest in animation, I did not actually begin drawing cartoons professionally until much later.

In 1976 I was introduced to Winston Jordan, a cartoonist from my home town in Barbados who taught me the basics of drawing facial expressions and the human figure. The thrill and opportunity of meeting Jordan, already an established animator, encouraged me to begin developing my own style. My dream was to be like Byron Payne, an animator for the Canadian Broadcasting Corporation, and to form my own special niche in the animation industry.

I had always wanted to move from the world of cartoons into that of full-fledged animation, but it was only when UNICEF presented the opportunity of formal training that I had the chance to take this step. In July 1991, UNICEF, in cooperation with Disney Feature Animation and the Jamaican Information Services, organised an animation training workshop in Jamaica at CARIMAC, the University of the West Indies. Since I had already become fairly well-known in Barbados for my cartoons, I was selected by UNICEF to participate in the workshop.

Eighteen artists from a number of different countries from around the world converged on Jamaica for the two-week workshop. We learned the art of animation. We learned how to make our characters walk, run, jump, bounce a ball, and ultimately move, which is the basic stepping stone to learning the trade of an animator. During the first week of training, each artist, all of whom were accomplished illustrators, designed a character that they felt could communicate social messages effectively in their individual countries. The artists were then shown how to colour and paint animation cels and how to construct a storyboard on a given theme. Each night, popular animated films were screened and discussed, highlighting the range of issues that could be covered by animation techniques.

During the second week of the workshop we produced a fifty-second spot in the form of a pencil test. The spot was about child abuse and its goal was to draw attention to this sometimes hidden problem. The spot, *Johnny Sad-Boy*, which could take place in any neighbourhood in the West Indies, shows a very sad and depressed young boy walking along the street. He is thinking about all of the bad things he goes through at home, where he is beaten and ill-treated. As he walks, he bumps into a woman on the street. The woman initially raises her arm as if to hit him, but she actually reaches out and pats him gently on the head. Johnny is elated because he realises that not everybody wants to hit children.

Johnny Sad-Boy or Child Abuse, as it was originally titled, was taken from the pencil test stage and completed at two additional training workshops held in Barbados. At the first of these workshops, Disney Feature Animation collaborated by sending their top ink and paint artist to conduct the training. It was during this week that we transferred the pencil test to animation cels and painted them in full-colour. At the last of the workshops, the head of Disney's training programme, Frank Gladstone, was on hand to show us how to use the camera and film the one-minute feature.

© UNICEF

Frank Gladstone of Disney training animators at the Jamaica Workshop in 1991.

The completed *Johnny Sad-Boy* was screened on television throughout nineteen countries in the Caribbean on UNICEF's International Children's Day of Broadcasting in 1993. It has since been shown regularly in the region as a public service announcement.

© UNICEF

Johnny Sad-Boy walking down the street.

In 1993, UNICEF asked me to submit a portfolio to Disney Feature Animation to be considered for a slot in their internship programme, reserved for an artist from a developing country. Up against stiff competition, my portfolio was selected. The four-month internship, which I completed in April 1994, was invaluable. During the programme, I was trained in every aspect of animation. It was a fantastic opportunity to really learn about the complete animation process — from storyboards to sketches to the final product.

The Disney internship programme was intense, and there were many challenging experiences throughout the months. As part of their requirements, Disney conducted a number of animation tests. I remember these as being one of the toughest parts of the entire training period. For example, in one test we were required to draw "in-betweens" for some of Disney's established characters like Mickey Mouse and Goofy. For this test, I would be given a series of three drawings, called "key drawings" or key positions, and I would then have to draw the in-betweens to create a smooth flow of movement.

As part of my final project for the internship, I produced a pencil test for a thirty-second spot on teenage pregnancy. After I returned to Barbados, I coloured and ultimately completed the spot on a computer animation system. Using a computer eliminated the time consuming process of hand painting each individual animation cel. The final animated piece on teenage pregnancy has since been used by UNICEF throughout the Caribbean.

One of the most rewarding aspects of the internship at Disney was returning to Barbados and knowing that I had been trained by some of the best animators in the world. I feel as though I have the confidence to approach and complete an animation project in the most economical way possible, as well as to deal with any animation problems that may arise throughout the process.

Most recently, I have begun working with UNICEF on a number of short animated films dealing with issues such as AIDS, teenage pregnancy, alcohol and drug abuse, and the importance of going to school. I feel very strongly about the power of animation to help communicate important social messages in the Caribbean. The continued success of *Johnny Sad-Boy* is an example of this. Animation can help children and families develop skills that enable them to cope with a number of problems. Because animation is well-received by children, it is also a good way to keep them informed of their rights as citizens. I take pride in the fact that by working with UNICEF on animation projects, I am working towards helping kids.

© UNICEF

Johnny Sad-Boy looking surprised when the woman pats him on his head rather than hits him.

© UNICEF

The happy family, to which Johnny Sad-Boy wishes he belonged.

Guy O'Neal is a Barbadian graphic designer, artist and animator and has assisted UNICEF on a number of animation and communication projects.

The Hiroshima Experience

Sayoko Kinoshita

Thirty years ago, I was among the many people who didn't know what animation was. Although I had graduated from an art college, it was only when I began to work for an animation production company in Tokyo that I became interested in this exciting medium. Since then, I have not only immersed myself in the world of animation, but have begun promoting and teaching the unique art form.

Together with my husband Renzo Kinoshita, I made my first animation film in 1971, entitled *What On Earth Is He.* The film is about the dangers of air pollution. The following year, we made another animated film called *Made In Japan*, which describes the unusual high growth of the economy in Japan during the early seventies. *Made In Japan*, which satirised the idea of people losing their humanity, won the Grand Prize at the New York International Animation Festival. Despite our success with these films, it was evident that animation as an art form had not yet attained the status and respect it deserved. We decided to expand our efforts beyond creating animation, and began developing and promoting the industry itself.

In order to make the animation industry more visible, Renzo and I organised an international animation festival in Japan. This festival would provide an opportunity for animators to meet one another as well as supplying an outlet for screening their work. Despite the experience we gained from attending other festivals, it took us twelve years of organisation and sponsorship efforts before Japan's first International Animation Festival was held in Hiroshima in 1985. Since then, the festival has been held biennially. The International Animation Festival in Hiroshima has provided an opportunity for films which may be considered slightly controversial or unconventional to be publicly screened. One such film is *No More AIDS*, which I made in cooperation with several artists in 1994 . The film was meant to be a requiem for colleagues who had passed away from the disease, as well as to highlight the issue of AIDS in Japan, where the disease is still not completely understood. If it had not been for the International Animation Festival, *No More AIDS* might not have been seen by so many people.

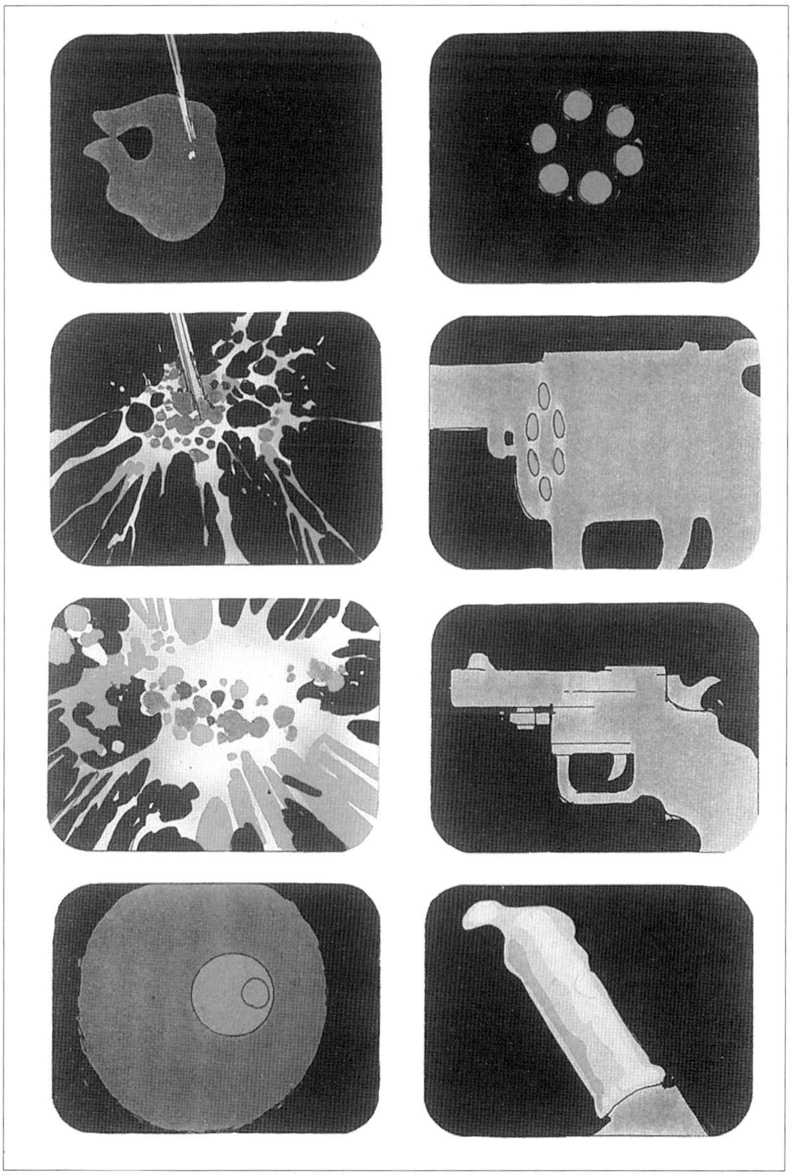

New Zealand animator Bob Stenhouse's storyboard contribution to *No More AIDs*

With the International Animation Festival now firmly in place, Renzo and I are planning to establish an Animation Institute in Hiroshima. We hope such an institute can expand and strengthen the animation industry in Japan. The envisaged institute will be open to students worldwide. When complete, it will provide studios for animation artists to create their work, as well as an archives library for both films and documents. We hope that the new Animation Institute, in conjunction with the biennial festival, will continue to strengthen the growth and development of animation as an art form and educational tool in Japan.

When I'm not working on these time consuming projects, I focus my attention on teaching animation to students, young and old, who already work in the field of visual media in Japan and in developing countries. I teach because I feel it's very important to demonstrate how effective animation is in extending beyond specific generations and languages.

As part of my teaching, I operate a number of workshops in developing countries in an effort to assist government departments in creating communication films. For example, one workshop might help a country's Ministry of Health teach people how to make animated films on vital issues such as AIDS or family planning. As a result of the workshops, the participants, even those with no prior experience in animation, can produce effective animated pieces on issues relevant to their specific regions and cultures.

In Japan, I run an annual workshop sponsored by the Japan International Cooperation Agency (JICA) in Okinawa, where professional people working in developing countries are invited to Japan for four to six months to study various media techniques. This workshop includes a programme on animation production, and includes screening a multitude of animated films, as well as exploring a variety of animation media. One task I give them is to describe the numbers zero through eleven using animation, similar to what's done on the children's educational programme, *Sesame Street*. I try to teach my students not just the techniques of animation, but also the professional procedures of production, so that they will be confident enough to begin creating their own animation when the workshop is over.

The animation programme is generally made up of ten to twelve participants from around eight developing countries, and the dynamics of the group depends on the skill level of the members. I try to adapt the course to fulfil the needs of all participants, whether they be beginners or experienced animators. I also think it's important to respect the participant's intention and originality regarding the theme, story and the animation materials developed and discussed throughout the class. Participants become more confident and eager about the art of animation when they have a chance to create something on their own, although I'm always available for assistance whenever it's needed.

Sayoko Kinoshita is an award-winning Japanese animator who founded and convenes the Hiroshima International Animation Film Festival.

An animation workshop at the Ministry of Health, Turkey.

The National Film School of Denmark

Gunnar Wille

The National Film School of Denmark has chosen to develop specialised education in animation to cater to the expanding production of animation films throughout the world. The European market could be a part of this global expansion, and the improvement of narrative techniques and the ability of producers to set new standards for international cooperation are key to this future.

The animation department at the National Film School of Denmark.

The National Film School of Denmark has a long and strong tradition for research on the narrative techniques of film. This is well reflected in the school's graduation films, which generate considerable interest and regularly win prizes at film school festivals throughout the world. By having an animation department at the Film School, we hope to supply the European animation community with an advanced knowledge of film language.

Students who are interested in the animation programme are subject to a demanding selection process, and eventually only four to six students will be accepted. The animation students are trained together with students of traditional film courses such as scriptwriting, live action directing, producing, film photography, sound design and film editing. They are also taught dramaturgy, editing techniques, sound engineering and producing. In turn, the general film students are exposed to animation through collaborations which hopefully will create an increased and concrete interest in animated film.

The National Film School of Denmark feels that to improve the art of animation, it must experience many of the changes that live action film has already passed through, specifically the dramaturgy concerning the manuscript, editing, music, sound and scenography. Not only must the new young directors be brought up with this knowledge, but those directors already established in the business should be educated in this area. Animators must come to realise that the development of strong narration is possibly the most important aspect of any good film, whether it be a television series, feature film or information/education film. If you can't keep the audience in front of the screen, your point will be lost.

There are various tools available for surveying how successful a film is in affecting the audience, and in the following pages I will break this down into a dramaturgic model which can be applied to all kinds of films. However, it is important to keep in mind that animated film is not based on its ability to mimic live action film, but does depend on using and adapting the elements of live action narrative to the specific dynamics of animation. For example, if you wish to describe a major inner conflict within a person, live action film generally handles this situation with an extreme close-up shot of the actor who expresses very complicated emotions through the eyes, small movements of facial muscles, etc. The human face is very expressive. However, if you wish to describe this same conflict in an animated film, you must use outer actions to get the same result. A face in an animation film can be as simple as a circle, two black dots (the eyes) , and a curved line (the mouth), so obviously the means of expression in this case are limited. Also, in animation, it is impossible to keep a close-up in many frames. Therefore, formal schools of animation must provide students with a model and guidelines for successfully developing and enhancing narration to provide alternative ways to convey these inner conflicts.

A Dramaturgic Model

The narrative film is divided into four parts of equal length. If, for example, you make a ten- minute film, each part will last approximately two-and-a-half minutes. Following is a breakdown of these four equal parts or "acts:"

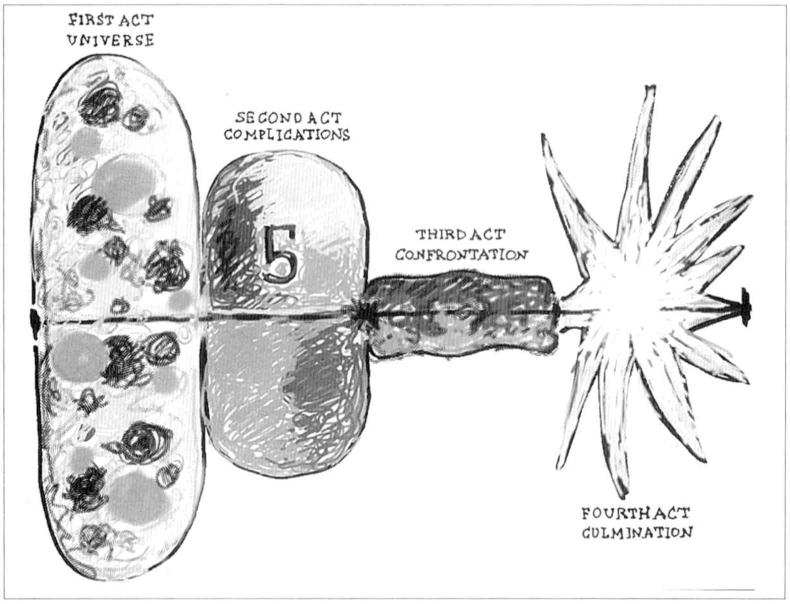

The Dramaturgic Model provides guidelines for animation students on successfully developing and enhancing narration.

First act: film universe

The entire world of the film is described during this initial act. The film language, such as the style of editing and sound design, is revealed. Locations, characters, and the time period in which it takes place is presented and described and the audience is given a sense of what the film will be about. In this first act, we meet a world as large as is possible, but at the same time it should limit the possibilities to those contained only in this particular story.

Towards the end of the first act, an event or incident should give a first inkling of the end of the film. For example, if the main character is to die a violent death, the first act must show violence, preferably involving a significant character. This lets the audience know that in this particular film, the main character may die. It is important to note that the film universe or world created during this first act cannot subsequently be altered. The introduction of new elements later in the film could cause a film to fall apart and lose credibility with the audience.

Second act: complications

In the second act of the film, the "complications" are presented to the audience. For example, if the subject is a little girl wishing to attend school, the complications revealed in this act might be: that she lives in a world where only boys can attend school, her parents tell her she only needs to know how to clean the house, or she is just a child and in this world, adults don't listen to children. There are usually no more than five of these complications within a film. In the second act, the film universe is reduced to fewer persons and places.

The second act generally ends with an event that brings the viewer into the very heart of the film, and this event usually occurs about halfway through the film. Using the above example, this event might be that the girl who wishes to go to school decides to go anyway, despite her parents' rules.

Third act: confrontations

In the third act, the story is confined to the main characters and it is at this time that we fully realise the true story of the film. Whereas in the first and second acts a universe with complications is presented, in this third act, the complications lead to a "confrontation." Using the above example of the girl who went to school despite her parents' wishes, this confrontation might be her parents' learning of her disobedience and being upset with her. Thus, the true story of the film turns out to be rebelling against family customs and traditions.

Fourth act: culmination

In the fourth act, we see the culmination or resolution of the tension created in the third act. Often, for dramatic effect, the story will appear to be resolving itself, just before exploding into a violent event which then fades down. What this violent event consists of is dependent on the kind of film in question. For example, in a Hollywood action film it may be a gigantic car chase, whereas in a Polish social film it may be as simple as a female character smashing a flowered coffee cup. All of the tension that was built-up throughout the third act is released in this culmination.

Tools of Dramaturgy

There are a number of tools which should be used in a live action or animated film to create a good story. These are: passion and will, the scene, the natural story, music, sound, and scenography. All of these elements are crucial to obtaining a result which is as vital and exciting as possible.

Passion and Will: A good story needs to have dramatic characters who possess "passion and will." The "passion" generally acts to force a person towards confrontation and release. An example of passion could be the wish to be alone, the desire be loved, or even the wish to die. A person may not always be aware of this desire, but it is vital to his or her way of life. The "will" is a person's conscious decision to act, such as solving a problem, clearing a murder, winning a fight, or even controlling the world. These wishes are often in contradiction with the person's desire, so logically this clash generally creates the drama in the film.

The Scene: Each scene in the film needs to maintain a connection with the principal characters and stories being developed. The process begins with introducing the audience to the contents of the scene which must be clear, dramatic and simple. Once this scene is presented, its complications are revealed. The composition of the scenes should contribute to the complexity of the story.

The Natural Story: A good narrative should use the physical surroundings within the film for the development of the story. By utilising the setting, the method of telling the story is facilitated. In turn, not using the surroundings within the context of the film may make them appear unnecessary in the development of action.

Music: Music is a useful narrative tool which not only enhances the story, but is a powerful vehicle with which to create atmosphere. Feelings of joy, sorrow, fear, and love can all enhanced by music, and therefore it must be chosen with the greatest care. The music for a film should be viewed as a symphony, having both peaks and low points rather than just a constant noise from start to finish. Music, if used the right way, can increase the possibility of operating within a larger and more exciting emotional range.

Sound: Sound may also be used in many ways throughout the film. It can emphasise details, add weight and body to characters, or even describe the surroundings. As with music, sound needs to be chosen with care and designed to work in close unity with the story. Sounds may also be integrated into the film as a symphonic course, having peaks and low points.

Scenography: Like music and sound, the scenography should be used as part of the story. One example of how this could be used as part of the drama is the use of colours within a scene. Using this strategy, perhaps there would be a scene where everything would be green: green fields, green houses, green woods, etc. When the dramatic peak is reached, perhaps all of the colours would now be shades of red.

Formalised Training

The formalised training in animation at the National Film School of Denmark includes a number of learning methods. The essential elements are a mix of theory, seminars, workshops and practical work. The theory portion of the training generally focuses on drawing, animation, and film analysis, accomplished through a combination of lectures, screening and analysis, and supplemented by short tests and practical exercises. In the seminars, students concentrate on a single subject, primarily through screenings, supplemented by lectures and interviews. The seminars are a joint learning process between film school students and teachers. Workshops generally feature guest speakers focusing either on current productions or on projects designed individually for the student. Lastly, all theories and skills are combined in a practical application, where students show their skills through a number of "pen-tests." These are the central tests in connection with the lectures on narrative structure and research into the basic film language.

Once students have received grounding in these elements of narration, they are given the opportunity to put theory into practice by developing their ideas into animatics, video segments of cartoon pieces that present a visual and audio sample of ideas. At the National Film School of Denmark, much of our practical training focuses on learning how to test different film theories using these short animatics. This process consists of creating smaller scenes within a film, such as an opening scene, a meeting, or the introduction of several people within a story.

First, the students make a short manuscript which will be converted into a rough storyboard. This storyboard is worked through and filmed into an animatic, which is then edited together with a simple sound track. At this early point it is possible for the students to analyse the course of their film. The stories are discussed in class, after which students generally rewrite their manuscripts. Several storyboard drawings are then made accordingly (approximately one drawing per second), and are filmed and edited into a new and final animatic. At the National Film School, we have found that this dialogue between manuscript, storyboard and animatic is the best way for the director to learn and understand how to use the rules of drama properly.

An animated illustration of characters created by Gunnar Wille.

As the animation programme at the National Film School of Denmark grows stronger, it is our hope that the animation industry in Europe will be bolstered and strengthened by an influx of talented animators armed with the tools to create new and compelling animated narratives.

Gunnar Wille is Head of Animation at the National Film School of Denmark. A well-known and accomplished author and illustrator of children's books, Wille has published over 22 titles in Denmark.

National Film School of Denmark Curriculum

During the first three semesters students currently attend lessons in dramaturgy (15 lessons per semester), film history (10 lessons per semester) and general educational subjects (10 lessons per semester).

The First Year

- Introduction to film analysis, storyboard, idea conception, drawing and animation
- Drawing lessons on ordinary objects, life, portrait and architectural drawing
- Introduction to basic use of cameras, sound equipment and editing tables
- Introduction to live-action vs. animation
- Film seminars
- Production of live-action editing exercises
- Production of 3 animatic "pen-tests"
- Introduction to the school's animation computers

The Second Year

- Film analysis, storyboard, idea conception, drawing and animation
- Photoartistic elements: lighting, composition and camera movements
- Introduction to animation film sound
- Introduction to individual directing and working with the actor
- Introduction to scriptwriting and structure
- Film seminars
- Production of 3 animatic "pen-tests"
- Production of a 10-minute animated story board on computer or film

The Third Year

- Film music for animation films
- Collaboration with a sound engineer on sound concepts
- Animation film production, including budgeting, financing, film studio visits
- Continuation of storyboard development
- Individual directing
- Collaboration between student and an animator from the Danish animation industry

The Fourth Year

- Development and completion of professional animation projects

SECTION THREE

Models

Successful Animation Projects

Bottom right: the first of 19 drawings used to create this short flip sequence which takes you to the chapter on the *Maximo* series.

Kids Deserve to be Heard

Geraldine Laybourne

In this chapter, I would like to explore how important it is for kids to be heard. They deserve to be heard. Before I came to Nickelodeon, I specialised in teaching media literacy and media-making with kids, and in researching films and television programmes directly with kids. As a teacher, I was convinced that kids could tolerate different art styles than what they saw on Saturday morning television in the United States. I was determined to prove my point. It has taken me about 15 years at Nickelodeon to get there, but today we are proving that kids like diverse art styles.

One of the most eye opening experiences I had during my pre-Nickelodeon days was in 1979 when I travelled to Singapore and Thailand with my husband Kit Laybourne, who was working on a United Nations generated project. It was the Year of the Child, a remarkable worldwide initiative sponsored by the United Nations. Under the UN's aegis, Kit had developed an idea—to have filmmakers travel around the world to work with kids and help them make films that reflected their own cultures and ideas. My husband and his colleagues simply provided the kids with the resources and technical assistance they needed in order to tell their own stories. The rest was up to them.

In Singapore, the kids were terrific at doing documentaries, probably due to their rich experience with television and government-sponsored films. They were all thumbs at animation. In Thailand, the kids found it difficult to work together in groups to make documentaries because that wasn't part of their history. However, they took to animation immediately, probably due to their strong tradition with shadow puppets. It was as if they had been waiting to speak out and tell their stories—they simply needed someone to give them permission and show them how. But in both countries, there was no question that given the chance, kids were capable of doing some pretty remarkable things.

Since 1984, when I became president of Nickelodeon, I've brought my commitment to listening to what kids have to say to every aspect of our network. This is particularly true of our innovative approach to animation. Conventional broadcasters in the United States thought we were taking huge risks by shunning the true and tried American Saturday morning approach, which is to base cartoons on pre-existing toys, movies, books or properties.

When Nickelodeon took the creator-driven new character route, we minimised our risk by involving kids in the process. This was the only way we would succeed with kids. We bring this commitment to kids' perspectives to bear in all of our animation programming decisions. We're proud of the many talented animators at Nickelodeon and the diversity of styles that they represent. This is certainly true of *Doug*, created by Jim Jenkins, who is so real that I'm certain this little 11-year-old boy lives inside of Jim's head everyday. Doug's adventures consist of everyday activities. He's a super-hero whose powers derive from the fact that he is decent and simply does the things that regular kids do—things that every kid can recognise and identify with. The unique animation style of the highly acclaimed series, *Rug Rats*, which looks at the world from the floor up the way a kid does, further illustrates our commitment to a kid's perspectives. Then of course there's the somewhat bizarre *Ren and Stimpy*, which has in some very fundamental way connected with kids.

What links all of these otherwise unique programmes together is that they all try to see the world with kid's eyes in a way that kids can relate to. This was not always true for Nickelodeon. When the network started in 1979, it was known as the "green vegetable network" and in fact my son, Sam, who was five years old at the time, told people I was a housewife because he was embarrassed that I worked there. He no longer lies, though. He's very proud.

Back then, we at Nickelodeon were not all "ears" as we try to be today. Instead we were all "voice." We were an adult voice and we were very loud. It's odd, because we tried to put on programming that we thought were good for kids, but we had a

split personality because we also thought we needed to use conventional advertising techniques to shout out to kids that this programming was fun. The theory was that if we said it loud enough and often enough, kids would believe we were fun. So I guess we shared with Sam that early lying ability. Now, we try to be more honest.

Nickelodeon's bizarre but kids-connected *Ren & Stimpy*

But in fact, the only people who loved Nickelodeon in the early days were parents. It seemed we were providing kids with exactly the type of programming that their parents thought they needed. In spite of our enthusiasm at Nickelodeon, we didn't get any ratings. We realized that in order to be truly successful, we had to open our ears to what kids had to say about us and about themselves.

It did not take long for us to realise that kids saw things differently from their parents and felt very differently about our programming, and so we began to incorporate the very first principle of Nickelodeon—that kids deserve to be heard and counted. An enormous amount of research was undertaken. We asked kids around the country just what they thought about Nickelodeon and why they weren't watching our shows. At first, this research was painful and embarrassing. Most kids thought that our shows were boring at best and preachy at worst. Kids were smarter than anyone had given them credit for, and they just didn't buy our hype. They didn't care how much fun we thought the programmes were or how much their parents wanted them to watch them. The truth was that there just wasn't much that we had to say that our young viewers were interested in hearing.

We also asked the kids in the research groups about themselves and the things that were important to them. Most importantly, we asked them what they most enjoyed about being kids. The answer was both disturbing and instructive. We found to our amazement that kids didn't really like being kids at all. They saw themselves as living in a world that was dominated by adult needs and opinions. They were terrified about things like teen pregnancy and drunk driving. They felt that no one cared about what kids had to say about how they felt or what they wanted. About the only positive thing they did say about being a kid was that they didn't yet have to face those teenage problems.

Many of them revealed to us that they were terrified of growing up. This was startling stuff. When I was a kid, I actually looked forward to all that. But we found that kids today face a very different world. We realised that if we wanted to speak with kids, we would have to listen more closely to what they had to say about themselves, their world and their experience with and expectations of the media. So we changed

Some characters from Nickelodeon's animated series *Real Monsters*

Nickelodeon's character Doug created by Jim Jenkins

The characters from Nickelodeon's highly acclaimed series *Rug Rats*

Nickelodeon's Clarissa in an episode from the series *Clarissa Explains It All.*

our thinking. We began to give kids what they said they needed most. We began to give them, on television at least, a place where they could get away from adults and their problems. A spot on the television dial where they could just be kids in a place that celebrated "kid-dom." Therefore, we actually ended up advertising kids and the state of "kid-dom" to themselves.

Armed with these insights, we did something radically different. We relaxed. We stopped hyping how much fun we were and we actually started having fun. We made a commitment to keep our ears open to what kids themselves had to say, to stay current with kid's views of the world and to deepen our understanding of their needs and their perspectives.

We still conduct 250 focus groups annually across the United States. We've learned that precocious cute-as-a-button children that populate most sitcoms and conventional children's programming, make most kids feel ignored and inadequate. Instead, what they most want to see are *real* kids on TV—kids just like themselves and their friends. We conducted a study on issues that affected children ages six through seventeen. It is the most comprehensive survey on kid's lifestyles and attitudes in the world. The data is gathered from 1,200 personal interviews, and we asked everything from how they make their friends to what they worry about.

Nickelodeon also connects with kids through computers and the information highway. We talk to some 150 kids on an almost daily basis everyday after school. If I have special questions, I can go on the network and talk to kids directly. This research has taught us that kids are eager to learn more about their world, and to play an active role in making it a better place to live.

Our commitment to empowering kids to tell us what they want is expressed most clearly in our "Declaration of Kids' Rights," which was drafted in 1990. The declaration restates the US Bill of Rights from a kid's perspective, affirming such fundamental kids' rights as being seen, heard and respected. The declaration's list of rights includes being treated like an equal no matter how small you are, being allowed to make mistakes, and openly expressing the way you think and feel, even when other people don't agree with you.

Nickelodeon has given kids a chance to be heard and to contribute to what they see and hear on our programmes. Now they expect to be heard, and the network may have actually created a little bit of a monster. But I take great pride in the fact that as the "boss lady of Nickelodeon" I now get furious letters from kids when they don't think that we are completely addressing their needs.

For example, I got a letter from a viewer who felt that there were not enough kid on-air hosts, and he reminded me that kids are people too. In another letter, a little girl complained that boys were winning more often on *Guts*, our fantasy sports show. We are very proud of the fact that we give equal opportunity for both girls and boys on all of our game shows, so I had the producer go back through the history of the game and give me a breakdown. It turned out that 52 percent of the winners were boys, compared with over 48 percent girls. Although I felt that was pretty darn close, I was thrilled that she was angry enough to write to me to complain. Which brings me to another component of our philosophy—kids deserve to be heard, even girls.

In many countries girls are treated not even as second class citizens, but as property. At Nickelodeon we have a strong commitment to demonstrate to girls that we listen to what they have to say. We learned early on that when programmers talked about kids and kids' issues, they usually meant boys. For years, the conventional wisdom was that kids, boys and girls alike, would respond positively to programming designed exclusively for boys. The broadcast industry seemed to feel that girls would watch anything, but that boys would not watch programmes that had girls at the centre of the action. Over the years, we at Nickelodeon have gone out of our way to challenge these myths. The response from our viewers has consistently proven us right.

The success of programmes like *Clarissa, Alice* and *Mac and Eureka's Castle*, have demonstrated that girls have been starving to see female characters portrayed and female issues explored in children's programming. It showed that boys—and they don't even mind admitting it—find these shows interesting as well. Armed with what we've learned from our young viewers, we've continued to defy the media's sacred cows about children's programming.

But the major aspect of our thinking—in fact, the basis of our philosophy—is that kids not only deserve to be heard, but empowered to question what they hear. We successfully challenged the previously untested assumptions that kids can't take straight information such as news orientated programming. We believed, and our research confirmed, that kids want to know more about their world. They deserve not to be spoon-fed sugar-coated information, but to learn how to question what they are told. They deserve to be empowered. As we've listened to kids over the years, we've learned that they do care about the problems and issues that impact their world. But in order to be heard, kids first have to be presented with the challenging information and to learn how to respond to it critically.

This is why I've always felt so strongly about our news programming. We give kids valuable up-to-date information and provide them with a context for questioning. By teaching kids to question what they see and hear about the world, including what they see and hear from us at Nickelodeon, we help to ensure that they'll refuse to settle for the simplistic answers that have increasingly come to dominate the political process in the United States.

Perhaps this will mean that ten years from now, when many of Nickelodeon's viewers are ready to vote, they will demand better candidates and more thoughtful solutions to issues that concern them. Perhaps twenty years from now, some of them will be prepared to be better candidates and leaders themselves, and to provide more sensitive and substantive solutions to problems that confront their communities and their world. During the 1992 US elections, Nickelodeon ran a poll in which kids could pick the candidate they wanted to be President of the United States. Over 12 million call attempts were made! This overwhelming response demonstrates how strongly kids feel about the political process.

The next step in realising Nickelodeon's commitment to empower kids involve using interactive media to connect kids to one another on television. We believe that kids deserve to be heard in "real time." To implement this, we've recently introduced an innovative program called *You to You*, which in a way takes us full-circle back to the experience my husband and I had in Singapore and Thailand. We invite kids to call, write, and even modem-in with suggestions that teams of animators, artists and musicians then bring to life on TV. In the UK, where we just started Nickelodeon, we have an all-morning programme called *Nick Alive*, which consists of live hosts who talk to kids via fax, modem and phone calls. *Nick Alive* has been hugely successful and is a window to the future of interactive media.

Lastly, we at Nickelodeon believe strongly that kids deserve to make a contribution. In 1994, we undertook a tremendous project called *Nickelodeon's Big Help*, the biggest social programme in our network's history. The project, supported by a $13 million budget, was designed to build a unique on-air relationship with kids by encouraging and empowering them to participate in community service activities. Celebrities like Whoopi Golberg and David Robinson joined the cause, and in fact, President Clinton opened the phone lines for a televised 12 hour "help-a-thon." During that time, 5 million kids called in and pledged 31 million hours of community service.

We want that message to get out to the adult world, because we believe kids do want to be connected. Nickelodeon believes that campaigns like the *Big Help* represent the future of interactive programming, through which kids and programmers work together to connect kids with one another and with the world around them.

The final thing I want to say is that we believe kids don't just deserve to be heard in the United States, but around the world. We think they deserve to be heard out into the future. And as Nickelodeon branches out around the world, the first thing we do in each country is to go out and talk to the kids. The second thing we do is go out and talk to the creative community. So I hope that we meet you on that journey.

Geraldine Laybourne is President and Chief Executive Officer of Nickelodeon and has been a key advocate for UNICEF's animation and communication initiatives.

Children's Television Workshop

Gregory J. Gettas

The genesis of *Sesame Street* and the Children's Television Workshop began in 1966. Joan Ganz Cooney was commissioned by the Carnegie Corporation in the United States to study whether television could be used for the education of preschool children. Following a series of national surveys and interviews, Ms. Cooney approached Carnegie with a proposal for a seemingly revolutionary new preschool television programme. Her ideas outlined a "wall-less" classroom that would seek to educate young children and help them prepare to eventually enter school by using the techniques and entertainment value of commercial television. The proposed series would not just be aimed at the traditional audience of white, middle-class children, but instead, one specifically designed to address the needs of rural and inner city poor. Further distinguishing Ms. Cooney's plan was her idea to base the series on an equal partnership between television producers, content specialists and researchers with each contributing to the series' on-going design and implementation.

In 1968, *Sesame Street* was thus born. Along with it came the Children's Television Workshop (CTW), an experimental, non-profit, self-supporting education and research orientated television production company. From the late 1960s to the present, *Sesame Street* has been broadcast in over 130 countries, either in its original English-language form, or in one of 14 different local language co-production versions. One important reason for *Sesame*

Street's success is the process upon which it is based—the collaboration between researchers, producers, and content specialists all working together in the same room. Now known as the CTW Model, this integration of varied professional disciplines is based on CTW's fundamental aim to be seriously educational and entertaining at the same time.

Research and development work on *Sesame Street* typically proceeds through several stages. Before commencement of production, for example, an educational advisory committee is formed. Made up of leading academics, child specialists, researchers, educators, and creative personnel, the committee's responsibility is to formulate, and eventually codify, a detailed statement of curriculum goals that will ultimately guide every segment produced during the course of the series.

In addition, formative research is conducted prior to the series production in order to study the media usage habits and demographics of the intended target audience. For example, competitive television programmes and various format ideas are examined.

Next, proposed scripts and storyboards are evaluated by the research and advisory staff. This is done prior to animation, live action or studio shooting. This involvement ensures that the educational content of each segment has been successfully incorporated by the series' writers. This is done for the simple reason that it is better to change a script at the beginning of the process than spend millions of dollars on a segment only to find upon completion that it doesn't work.

However, endless amounts of pre-production research is useless unless, ultimately, the target audience watches

Kippi Ben Kipod (Israel) in *Rechov Sumsum*

Sesame Street, enjoys what they're seeing, and most importantly, is learning from it. It is for this reason that at the heart of the CTW Model is an ongoing emphasis on continual field testing. After completion of individual segments or completed episodes, the *Sesame Street* research staff constantly observes and probes the young viewers to determine what they like and don't like—when they laughed, clapped, sang along, or repeated phrases or words. Simultaneously, comprehension studies are also conducted to determine the educational effectiveness of the material produced. In other words, are the children actually learning? Once this

Dr. Valerie Lovelance, Director of Research for *Sesame Street*, works with children on the show.

data is collected from the field, it is analysed and passed along to *Sesame Street* producers, writers and directors in an attempt to constantly improve the series' appeal and educational effectiveness.

Finally, post-broadcast evaluations are also undertaken to determine whether *Sesame Street* has accomplished its stated objectives. Children are pre-and post-tested to measure cognitive achievements and gains in the series' stated goal areas. The results of this information are then sent back to the producers as they begin preparations for subsequent seasons.

Because of the inherent flexibility and scope of the CTW Model, it is widely incorporated by producers of children's television programming around the world. They recognise in it a methodology that is neither doctrinaire or culture-bound; one that can be freely adapted to achieve

different educational results in different countries.

The clearest indication of this adaptability can be seen in local language versions of *Sesame Street* that CTW has co-produced with broadcasters in Europe, North, Central and South America, the Middle East and the Pacific Rim. The International Production Department of CTW works with broadcasters around the world in order to bring local versions of *Sesame Street* to their country's children. Regardless of the nation in which CTW finds itself, the fundamental objectives remains the same—to help create local co-productions of *Sesame Street* that educate and entertain simultaneously and which fully incorporate the unique cultural, social, linguistic and educational needs of the specific country involved. The International Production Department doesn't aim for children's programming stamped with the words "Made in the United States," but rather, "Made in Kuwait," or "Portugal," or "The Netherlands."

In spite of their vast cultural, linguistic, religious and geographical differences, each country that chooses to work with CTW has been motivated to produce their own edition of the series for similar reasons. Each country, for example, places fundamental importance on the role of children and families in their societies. As a result, they all place the goal of improving education of young children among their highest national priorities.

Another reason international producers and educators have been drawn to *Sesame Street* is because of CTW's ability to provide maximum latitude in the production of each series. Rather than encouraging clones of the American original, we continually encourage local broadcasters to fully represent their own children and their own needs in each adaptation.

To accomplish this, each country organises and chairs their own *Sesame Street* curriculum seminar which, over the course of four days, establishes the educational objectives of each production. Following these seminars, each country then develops their own unique curriculum goal statement, conducts their own formative research, and begins the production process. Local producers, researchers, directors and writers are hired. And while all versions do utilise some material from CTW's international segment library, each *Sesame Street* adaptation has their own indigenous scripts, human casts, puppets sets, locally produced animation segments, studio shooting and live action films. For example, rather than the puppet character, "Big Bird," the star of the American version, Israel's *Rechov Sumsum* features "Kippy Ben Kipod," a prickly-on-the-outside, sweet-on-the-inside porcupine, who reflects the Israeli sabra. In the Arabic series, *Iftah Ya Simsim*, the principle character is "No-man," a camel puppet that is obviously drawn from local and native culture and history. Both the "Kippy" and "No-man" characters are extremely popular.

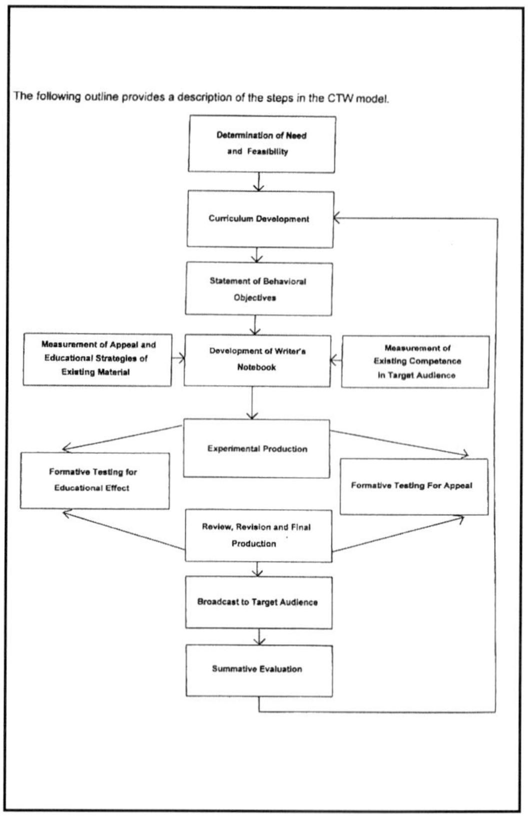

The Children's Television Workshop Model.

Studio sets for the series change from country to country as well. Rather than replicating the American street, which is the main set for the US version, Germany's set for *Sesamstrasse* consists primarily of a park. In Norway's, one of CTW's newest partners, they decided to shoot their series in a train station and had wonderful results.

As part of CTW's relationship with international producers, emphasis is placed on the production of locally-produced animation and live-action segments rather than American products. This provides each series with a sense of national "place" and enables it to meet local curriculum needs. In fact, these segments have become so good, CTW has begun to purchase some of them from our local broadcaster partners for inclusion in CTW's own international segment library. In fact, some of the spots are now being aired on the American *Sesame Street*.

The uniqueness of each *Sesame Street* series is distinguished by the curriculum goals involved, each formulated in different ways and for different reasons, depending on the country. To begin with, there is the question of need. For example, does this version of *Sesame Street* intend to better prepare children to enter school? The answer, of course, depends on the educational system in that country. For example, in The Netherlands, Germany, Norway and Spain, children go to preschool at an early age. So, in their versions of the series, the emphasis is placed more on emotional and social learning. In comparison, in Turkey, Portugal and the Arab world, where formal education does not begin at an early age, more emphasis is placed on specific cognitive learning objectives like counting and the alphabet.

As one might assume, there are also considerable differences in national curriculum objectives from country to country. For example, CTW's Canadian partner focuses primarily on French and English bilingual education, ecology and an awareness of differences amongst its many different multi-cultural groups. Latin American's *Plaza Sésamo* and Turkey's *Susam Sokagi* both place emphasis on the areas of health and hygiene. In the Israeli series *Rechov Sumsum*, considerable attention is given to life in the modern world, yet an equal amount is devoted to appreciation of the country's diverse cultural groups. *Rechov Sumsum* features children from different backgrounds, religions and walks of life including Arabs, Sephardic Jews, native-born citizens and immigrants. As preparations are made for a fifth series, they're actively inviting Palestinian participation as well, both in terms of curriculum, and as a means to help develop a Palestinian broadcasting infrastructure. The updated series will include Palestinian writers, will commission films shot in Gaza and the West Bank, and will incorporate the new characters into the series' regular cast.

CTW believes strongly in thc notion of training and transfer of technology. Rather than passively sell or distribute programmes, whenever and wherever asked, CTW helps train production teams in an effort to establish or enhance local broadcast capabilities as required by the country involved. For example, CTW offers hands-on training in the areas of formative research, organises seminars to help new writers polish their craft, holds directorial and technical workshops, helps find, select and train local puppeteers, and provides assistance in any other area the broadcasters request. Throughout the process, the selection and growth of an entire new generation of producers, writers and researchers takes place. Local productions of *Sesame Street* continue to expand. For example, during 1995 and 1996 local productions of *Sesame Street* will begin in Russia, China and Poland. Each of these countries chose to work with *Sesame Street* not just because of its educational value, but also because it is a means to develop creative capacities. It is an exciting prospect for these countries and one in which all partners can learn and share from the experience.

The global success of *Sesame Street* and the CTW model has proven that television can communicate without geographical boundaries while simultaneously preserving, protecting, and indeed, celebrating one's national culture. Yet, even more than that, television can be used to educate children, promote their well-being and help protect their fundamental rights. No one does that better than UNICEF. By working together, as we have recently accomplished through the production of *Plaza Sésamo*, CTW honours UNICEF's commitment and stands ready to further our mutual mission throughout the world.

Gregory J. Gettas is Vice President / Executive Producer of International Production at Children's Television Workshop.

Animation Nation: A Grassroots Approach to Social Interactivism

Abby Terkuhle

From the beginning, MTV has been an interactive medium. It's not a technology thing — it's the way viewers are young, demanding, opinionated and vocal. They let us know what they want and how they feel. And we listen. Which is how this whole pro-social thing came about, and why animation is such an appropriate and effective pro-social tool for us to utilise.

Early on we realised that MTV's On-Air Promotion department could and should be used for more than just promoting our shows and our image. We were getting a lot of feedback at the grassroots level — from our viewers and employees, not to mention all the artists and musicians we deal with. They were concerned about how people treated the earth and how they treated each other; issues that have moved young people from Woodstock to Bangladesh to Live Aid.

Of course, we've always felt that rock music, with its implicit themes of love, hope, tolerance and celebration, is a force for good. But now people were suggesting we become more specific. As we announced in a public television documentary called *MTV: The Reagan Years*, "The music of MTV accompanied a decade of endless partying, mindless waste and immediate gratification, most of it by rich old white people. Now, in the spirit of rock and roll, a new generation is trying to clean up the mess."

But there was a problem. How do you send a message that provokes thought and action without sounding preachy and teachy, which would be deadly for our audience? Grassroots animation proved to be a powerful solution. Like much of MTV, we let the people speak for themselves.

In our *Fact/Act* environmental campaign back in 1988 when I was still part of the demographic, we commissioned the work of twenty-eight young animators from around the world. Later we opened it up further with storyboard competitions for our *World Problems, World Solutions* and *Free Your Mind* campaigns. Most recently, as part of our *Enough is Enough* campaign, we asked prisoners to contribute their thoughts, poetry and artwork for spots against violence.

Animation at the local level turned out to be a great vehicle for promoting social causes in a non-didactic way. It has a high emotional impact and it helps you see things in a new way. It has a kind of "built-in" entertainment value that grabs your attention. It's very MTV — we've been doing animation since our first station identification. And it's very grassroots — an animator with just a few tools can send a message directly from his heart to the television screen.

A good example of emotionally charged animation is a *Free Your Mind* spot called

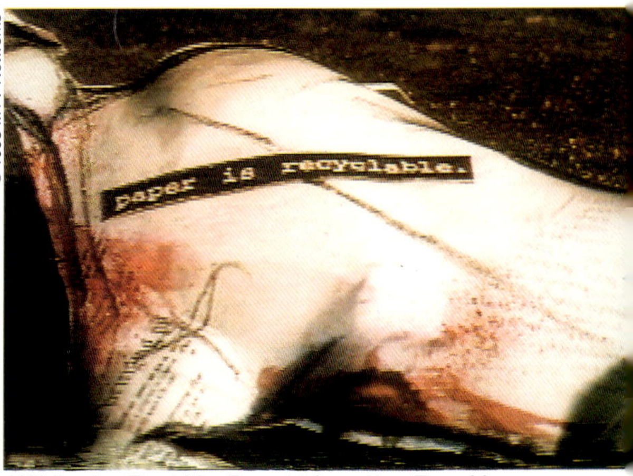

Wilding by Fred MacDonald from the *Free Your Mind* campaign

Wilding, directed by Fred McDonald and produced for us by Olive Jar Animation in Boston. It's basically an eerie, Zapruder-like recreation of the Rodney King and Reginald Denny beatings using paper figures and stop-motion photography. It ends with the message, "Paper is recyclable. People aren't. Free Your Mind." It's particularly effective, I think, because it takes images we've all seen a thousand times and puts them in a new context. The spot not only provokes our feelings, but hopefully our thoughts and our ability to see the greater meaning of the event.

Another *Free Your Mind* spot called "2 Devils," by animator Ben Smallridge, grabs the emotions in a simple, repetitive way that is almost musical. The result is something between whimsy and terror. Two devils are drinking at a bar. One says, "We've been doing this for years — shall we give it a go?" The other says, "Okay. On your mark, get set, go." They face each other and start repeating the phrase "I hate you" in unison.

With each repetition their images change into historic enemies. A black man and a white man. "I hate you." A Christian and a Jew. "I hate you." A businessman and Native American. "I hate you." An old woman and a young woman. "I hate you." Two gang members. "I hate you." Two Klansmen. "I hate you."

Finally — this is the high impact part — they become devils once again and look directly into the camera. "I hate you."

Emotional impact can be a tricky business, especially when you're trying to promote tolerance and non-violence. You don't want the thing to misfire. You want people to reflect as much as react. In a way, you're using emotion to defuse. For example, a spot we did called "Moment of Glory," really succeeded in making the viewer look at the problem of kids and guns in a new way. And it used a new kind of animation.

"Moment of Glory" was an experiment. MTV was approached by R. Greenberg, an animation production company in New York, and Soft-Image of Montreal to create a piece utilising a new motion capture technique they had developed. Two of our staffers, Todd Mueller and David Felton worked with Greenberg and came up with a spot that hopefully deglamorised guns and alerted people to the tragedy of young gun violence.

In the spot, two innocent-looking boys approach each other in a playground at night. It's surreal — like they're in a movie. They argue, but you can't hear the words. One boy pulls out a gun and then the other does the same, and at that moment they turn into chalk figures, shooting each other and collapsing to the ground. From above, the camera pulls back to reveal similar chalk figures covering the playground. Superimposed are the words, "Every two days in America enough young people are killed by guns to fill a classroom."

Of course not all of our pro-social promos are so heavy. After all, animation used to be called cartoons and has traditionally been a vehicle of humour and entertainment. And we've run some pretty funny stuff. Animator Lauren MacMullen did an environmental spot called "Feet" that is reminiscent of early Max Fleischer. To a jazzy 1930s track, a machine plops out automobiles driven by cartoon creatures. The cars create pollution and congestion, until finally a cow jumps out of her auto and yells, "Get out of your cars!" All the creatures get out, discover their feet and start walking and dancing. It's silly and right to the point.

Another animator, Bob Sabiston, did a piece where this irresponsible young person, probably an MTV viewer, ignores a recycling bin and dumps his old newspapers on the street. Immediately a huge tree picks him up and destroys him, leaving just his bloody shoes and a note: "Recycle. We mean it! — the Trees." Violent, but you know, *cute.*

In one of our cleverest *Free Your Mind* spots, "The Golden Calf" by Brian Mulroney, a bearded fanatic, apparently some kind of Judeo-Christian, walks through the hills carrying two holy tablets. Over the next hill, he spots a golden calf being worshipped by an unseen throng. He runs to the top of the hill and berates the throng, claiming his tablets are superior to the pagan calf. Then, to his chagrin, he notices the throng is made up entirely of golden calves. Cut to message: "Intolerance is bull."

But more than anything else, animation, like rock and roll, is an art form of and for the masses. It doesn't take a lot of money, or formal schooling, or rigid rules to produce. You just have something to say. A few years ago at MTV we started something called "Lab Time." Any On-Air Promo producer or production assistant could book a few hours each week at an edit house just to experiment. A young production assistant named Lisa Rubisch — today she's a producer but back then she'd been with us just six months — used her Lab Time and a title camera to superimpose various objects over a drawing of a female body. You know, things like tomatoes, door knockers, meat, a fish, a jackhammer, and faces of a pig, a cow and a bird.

The result was a brilliant spot against sexism that included, to the tune of Battle Hymn of the Republic, the following female voice-over:

> " We the people should be treated equally, regardless of size of chest or lack thereof, pertness of breasts, firmness or bounty of buttocks, frequency of intercourse, percentage of body fat or cellulite, length of hair, propensity towards shopping, height of heel, length of nose or circumference of thighs."

In 1991, MTV and MTV Europe conducted our first large-scale experiment in grassroots animation — an animated storyboard competition called *World Problems, World Solutions*. Animators from around the world were invited to submit storyboards which explored issues of global significance such as the deteriorating environment, prejudice and censorship. The creative challenge here was to focus on *solutions*, not just problems. The storyboards were judged by a panel drawn from the animation, music and education fields. Winning boards were each given the same production budgets, and the ten winners, including the work of Sabiston and MacMullen, were aired globally on MTV.

Feet by Lauren MacMullen, from the storyboard competition *World Problems, World Solutions*

Paper Doll, by Lisa Rubisch

The following year, MTV launched a channel-wide pro-social campaign focused on the issues of diversity and discrimination. This second storyboard competition was called *Free Your Mind*, and we asked animators to examine discrimination based on three factors: race and ethnic origins, religion and personal beliefs, and gender and sexual orientation. We received over one thousand storyboards worldwide, including "The Golden Calf" and "2 Devils" described above.

The Golden Calf by Brian Mulroney from the *Free Your Mind* campaign

One thing that struck me about these storyboard entries was how many of them used no words at all, which made them particularly appropriate for a visual medium like MTV. In Bruce Woodside's "Wake Up Call," a sleeping man awakes and sees a giant lit fuse in the sky. He wakes up other sleepers and tells them but they just laugh at him. He runs around the world, fruitlessly alerting sleepers, and now we see that the globe is actually a bomb to which the fuse is attached.

In "Symbols," by Tom Megalis, different religious believers fight over a monument, trying to change it to a Buddha, a cross and a Star of David. Finally, a lightning bolt from the sky turns it into a peace symbol. In "The Ruling Hands," by Sarah Roper, huge fingers from the sky force peaceful people on both sides of an ocean to war with each other. At the last minute, the people shoot the hands, bringing peace to the world.

On the other hand, words certainly were a part of our most recent grassroots animation experiment, the *Inmates Against Violence* project. We sent entry forms to inmates in three New York State prisons and asked them to submit drawings and writings. The forms read in part:

> " MTV's *Enough is Enough* campaign focuses on the impact of violence in our lives. This campaign hopes to affect all members of our society through special programming, MTV News coverage, Public Service Announcements, and events with artists as well as community and political leaders.

" Many of you are in prison because you've had first-hand experience with violent crime. Or maybe you, your friends, or family have been victims of violence. You've seen and felt the effect of violence. Now here's a chance for you to speak out against it, to millions of young people, on MTV.

" If you like to draw, write or both, use this entry form and send us your drawing and/or message. MTV will select material from the best drawings and most expressive writing to put together a series of 15-second Public Service Announcements (PSAs) against violence. The PSAs will run on MTV, nationwide."

Even the judging for the competition was grassroots. We asked employees in all departments of MTV to vote on the entries. The winning material was then assembled into promos by staff producers.

Strictly speaking I suppose, the *Inmates Against Violence* spots might not be considered animation. But in many ways, I think they represent our most successful attempt at grassroots interactivism. Paper and pencil were the only tools required, but these pieces speak directly from heart to heart and mind to mind.

In "Moon," by Chris, a 35-year-old writer and illustrator, the camera pans across a drawing of a night sky seen through prison bars. We hear a voice saying, "Many years have passed correcting my mistakes. Still I see the quiet sleeping moon every night from these heavy iron bars. It reminds me not to ever hurt anyone with violence."

In "Conspiracy," written by Gregory, 39, and illustrated by Bennie, 29, we see a field of guns, knives, needles and bottles controlled by giant hands in the sky. A voice reads an angry poem:

There's a conspiracy going on affecting our
  lives
The TV, our music, promoting the lie
Tell these big corporate guys with money to
  spend
Stop promoting violence from their end

"Culture," written by Kiekton, 28, with another drawing by Bennie, has a more conciliatory tone. It shows people of all races holding up an anti-weapons banner, while we hear these words:

From your culture to my culture
From my ethnicity to your ethnicity
Violence has pervaded our lives like the air
  we breathe
Denounce all forms of violence
Breathe safely again

All the *Inmates Against Violence* promos ended with the words, "Currently serving sentences at correctional facilities. Enough is enough."

Trees by Bob Sabiston from the storyboard competition *World Problems, World Solutions*

I find these kinds of grassroots animation encouraging for one more reason, perhaps the most important one. We discovered that social causes produce great creative results. Artists, animators and writers seem particularly inspired and liberated when the topic is not commercial, but social in nature. That should give us all some hope.

Abby Terkuhle is Senior Vice President and Creative Director at MTV where he executive produces all of MTV's animated fare, including station promos and the strip *Beavis and Butthead.*

Rights from the Heart

Francine Desbiens

The Convention on the Rights of the Child was adopted by the UN General Assembly on November 20, 1989. It consists of 54 articles detailing the individual rights of all persons under the age of 18. It states that children have the right to develop their abilities to the fullest without suffering from hunger, poverty, negligence, exploitation, or any other forms of injustice.

To bring attention to the importance of the Convention, the National Film Board Of Canada (NFB) began production on a series of films dealing with the rights outlined in this charter. The resulting series, *Rights from the Heart,* was conceived by the NFB's French Programme Animation Studio with the support of the Canadian International Development Agency (CIDA), Canadian Heritage and Health Canada. The series consists of three parts, aimed respectively at children ages five through eight, nine through twelve, and thirteen through eighteen. Each part of the series is made up of seven films — six of them dealing with a specific right and the seventh looking at the Convention in general. The films were produced by Thérèse Descary and directed by a multitude of filmmakers, making *Rights from the Heart* a truly collaborative collection.

At the onset of this film project, several discussions took place with the filmmakers to develop production guidelines. It was first decided that these films would be part of a "collection" (as opposed to a series), and therefore, the different animators should work in the tradition of the National Film Board, which encourages *"film d'auteurs"* or individual styles and the utilisation of varied animation techniques. Although the films would have specific guidelines concerning content, running time, and production deadlines, there was much room for personal insight from the filmmakers concerning the overall film style. As a result, the production process was extremely satisfying for the filmmakers — they were able to create films dealing with important issues, yet they were given the chance to express themselves in their own individual style.

It was determined that *Rights from the Heart* would be non-verbal so it could be readily available in the six official languages of the UN (English, French, Spanish, Arabic, Russian and Chinese). This enables the films to be used in classrooms and homes all over the world. However, we did feel it was important that these films were made with a Canadian audience in mind, and applied the Convention on the Rights of the Child to the children of Canada. We needed to recognise that although Canada is an industrialised country, many of our children dealt with huge problems and difficulties and didn't enjoy any of the well-being and comfort of our modern world. Poverty, hunger, child abuse and abandonment are all problems that our children may encounter. These can be very painful in an environment where money, competition, success and power are keys to happiness. These themes were the basis for the films in the collection.

Part 1 consists of films made for the youngest group of children. For this group, we chose to focus on articles of the Convention most applicable to small children — the right to eat, to have a family, to have learning aids, to be protected from abuse, to be heard and the right to healthy play. The series includes the following films:

• *Porte À Porte/Door to Door* (Director, Zabelle Côté) is set among children in a schoolyard and explores the right of children to be respected. *Door to Door* looks at young children in primary school being bullied by someone stronger, bigger or more powerful, and encourages children to defend themselves against harassment and ask adults to help in solving the problem.

• *Papa* (Director, Michèle Pauzé) is a sweet, simple story highlighting the right of children to be heard. In *Papa,* a young child seeks her father's attention, eventually getting the response she needs.

• *L'Orange/The Orange* (Director, Diane Chartrand), a story about a hungry school boy, signals the right of children to eat as much as they need. The film follows a young child suffering from hunger and teaches children that they cannot ignore poverty.

• *Une Famille Pour Maria/A Family For Maria* (Director, Lina Gagnon) is the story of a young homeless girl who lives on the street. She eventually finds love and acceptance in an adopted family, emphasising that all children have the right to a family.

• *1,2,3 Coco* (Director, Pierre M. Trudeau) is about children having the right to learn with dignity. Coco, a young school girl, is patiently taught by a caring teacher, and gains the confidence and courage to overcome her fears and realise she too has the ability to learn.

• *T.V. Tango* (Director, Martine Chartrand) deals with the effects violence in television programmes can have on children. The film reinforces a child's right to wholesome and creative play.

• *Voir Le Monde/To See the World* (Director, Francine Desbiens) emphasises that all the children of the world should have the same rights. In this film, we see a young boy travelling on a train ride around the world, witnessing the misery and injustice that children everywhere endure, realising that children everywhere deserve to be happy.

Because of the young target audience for Part 1, we felt it was important that viewers were provided with solutions to the problems raised in the films. In Parts 2 and 3 of *Rights from the Heart*, issues are not necessarily resolved, nor does every film have a happy ending.

Part 2, aimed at children ages nine through twelve, deals with more complex issues than those raised in Part 1. This group of films focuses on issues such as children at war, child labour, gender equality, racial equality, street children and physically disabled children. These films generally end with a question — why or why not? Part 2 includes the following films:

• *Jonas et Lisa/Jonas and Lisa* (Directors, Zabelle Côté & Daniel Schorr) looks at the right to an adequate standard of living, as told by the story of children who live in a slum and have to make adult decisions.

• *Le Tournoi/The Tournament* (Director, Francine Desbiens) highlights the right of physically or mentally disabled children to enjoy a full and decent life. The film tells the story of a young deaf girl who is unable to hear the boasting of her opponent and so beats him in a chess tournament.

• *Ex-Enfant/Ex-Child* (Director, Jacques Drouin) looks at the article in the Convention which states that children under fifteen should not be recruited into the armed forces. This right is portrayed through the story of a young boy taken away to fight in a war and as a result, loses his childhood.

• *Une Artiste/An Artist* (Director, Michèle Cournoyer), highlights a child's right to develop talents and abilities to their fullest potential. *An Artist* tells the story of a young girl who manages to compose music without the support or knowledge of her family.

• *Overdose* (Director, Claude Cloutier) looks at the right to leisure and rest through the life of a young boy whose parents keep him so busy he no longer has time for himself.

• *Baroque 'N Roll* (Director, Pierre M. Trudeau) tells the story of a young immigrant who is teased by other children until his courage finally wins their respect. It demonstrates that children belonging to minority groups have the right to enjoy their own culture, religion and language.

• *Pourquoi?/Why?* (Director, Bretislav Pojar) synthesises a number of children's rights, showing children urgently asking adults to do something about the hardships faced by children around the world.

The last part of the *Rights from the Heart* collection is targeted at teenagers from thirteen through eighteen. In early 1995, producers and topics for the seven different films were selected, and production is underway. Part 3 films are being co-produced with animators from several different countries, including Canada, India, Cuba, Czech Republic and Burkina Faso. The goal of this collection is to reinforce the concept of freedom — freedom of religion, freedom to marry, freedom of expression and freedom from addiction and abuse. This last group of films include the following:

• *Le Chapeau/The Hat* (Canada, Director, Michèle Cournoyer) deals with the right of children to be free from sexual exploitation. It tells the story of a young woman who

L'Orange, Diane Chartrand

Baroque'n Roll, Pierre M. Trudeau

Overdose, Claude Cloutier

Pourquoi? Bretislav Pojar

decides never to work again as a nude dancer after she has a flashback of an early incest experience.

• *Le Joueur De Cora/The Cora Player* (Burkina Faso, Director, Cilia Sawadogo) looks at the right of a child to have an opinion. *The Cora Player* deals with a young girl's conflict with her father, who won't accept her boyfriend because he is from another social caste.

• *Masques/Masks* (Cuba, Director, Elisa Rivas) deals with freedom of thought, conscience and religion. The film tells the story of a young man who refuses double standards imposed by his family.

• *La Lune À La Fenêtre/The Moon At The Window* (India, Director, Vishnu Mathur) also deals with the right to freedom of thought and religion. It shows the lives of children whose parents interrupt their schooling and oblige them to march in a religious demonstration.

• *Le Cadenas/Locked* (India, Director, Bhimsain) deals with the issue of child labour. *Locked* tells the story of a young boy who is denied the right to an education and to play because he must earn a living working in a factory.

• *Le Duel/The Duel* (Czech Republic, Director, Pavel Koutsky) looks at the implications of denying freedom of expression.

• *Narco Blues* (Czech Republic, Director, Ivan Vit) deals with the right to be protected from drug abuse, looking at a young man who enjoys his drug-induced hallucinations until he finds himself sucked into a vortex of criminality.

Part one of *Rights from the Heart* has been available on video since 1992 and part two became available in January 1995. We hope to complete the third grouping of films in 1997. Their main purpose is an educational tool in learning institutions throughout Canada and the world. Each collection of *Rights from the Heart* has an accompanying resource guide to provide teachers with a background on the rights portrayed in the films and a solid approach to presenting them, as well as a list of complementary activities to encourage true understanding of the messages provided. To this day the films from *Rights from the Heart* have won seventeen prizes in various International Film Festivals.

Francine Desbiens has been a film director at the National Film Board of Canada's French Animation Studio since 1971 and directed *Voir Le Monde* and *Tournoi* from the *Rights from the Heart* Collection.

Computer Gaming

Kit Laybourne

In 1979, I wrote a book called *The Animation Book*, which is a complete guide to animated filmmaking, from flip-books to sound cartoons. Almost 60,000 copies of the volume have made their way into the classrooms and studios and garages of people who love animation in all its forms and who want to know how to make their own. *The Animation Book* grew out of a set of notes that kept evolving during the ten years right after college that I spent working in schools and with teachers. I had three fundamental reasons for doing the book and these seem to have struck a responsive chord.

First, I found that there was a need out there for information about low-cost, low-tech approaches to animation. Secondly, while it was hard enough to see a wide range of animated movies, it was almost impossible to gain access to the "stuff" by which such movies were made — i.e. the working techniques, the tools and set-ups, and the planning and design artifacts behind various kinds of animation. Lastly, I found that people were hungry to meet animators, both those who worked in the studio system that created the classics of cel animation, as well as those who were, at that time, a part of a fledgling renaissance in independent animation. By this, I mean movies made by individual artists about topics that were intensely personal in impact.

These same needs are very much alive today. The Second Animation for Development Workshop under UNICEF's able leadership was a sign of that. The presence of so many animation studios and individual animators was another indication that The Renaissance continues. So, of course, is the robust health of the global box office for animated features and the healthy range of animated shows we see today on broadcast and cable television.

My own book, a tiny herald, continues to evolve too. *The Animation Book* is currently in metamorphosis into an interactive, CD-ROM tutorial about animation. This is a project I've undertaken with the Voyager Company, an acknowledged leader in the emerging field of multi-media publishing. We're aiming to create a new set of tools that will yield spirited expression by the next generation of digital animators.

Blockheads, by Eli Noyes and Mark Swain from MTV's *Liquid Television*

Computer Animation

In the next page or so, I'll give a quick and dirty introduction to computer animation. As most of you undoubtedly know, the amazing computational and rendering powers of the computer have already changed the face of animation. Let me begin with a catalogue of ways that computers provide support to the traditional aesthetic and production tasks that reside in making any piece of animation. My list has six items:

STORYBOARDING (& SCRIPTING): With any of dozens of drawing/illustration computer programmes, even using the most primitive computer, a designer can quickly compile a sequence of sketches that births most animated films. Faxes and modems make it possible to distribute and give close study to a storyboard. One can muster a better brain pool.

ANIMATICS: A number of software packages make it easy to make animatics, complete with timed voice tracks or music tracks. Animatics are also a valuable tool in eliciting feedback from audiences, clients, and creative collaborators.

PENCIL TESTS: The familiar Lyon-Lamb style video camera and light stand can be fused with or replaced by a scanner or digitising camera that records hand drawn images. When mounted into a digital format, it's easy to alter the speed and timing of scratch animation, or to edit the sequence and model screen transition effects.

INK & PAINT: In this method, registered drawings are scanned (done on Acme or Oxberry Bond) into the computer. Then, individual drawings are cleaned-up and then colourised, using standard programs with customisable colour pallets.

INBETWEENING: Given two key drawings, there are a number of computer programmes that will compute and render inbetweens, or the images remaining between two drawings to create the illusion of smooth movement. This is often done on basis of duration (number of intervening drawings) or of paths (spatial placement along a pre-determined vector). Note, however, that idiosyncratic application of stretch & squash (or "anticipation" and "exaggeration") is something that requires frame-by-frame design. I understand that new programmes are expanding the creative parameters of inbetweening.

LOGOS (GRAPHICS & TYPOGRAPHY): Computers have unparalleled powers to custom design print and graphic images. There are many books about desktop publishing and graphic design that have great value for animators.

Computers are, of course, their own art form. It is far too early for any of us, I believe, to have more than a very sketchy sense of the new kinds of animation that will evolve from these new tools. Here are eight self-distinguishing formations in the emerging landscape:

PATH ANIMATION: Don't be deceived by the flying logos that are already a cliché in film and broadcast graphics. There are many creative potentials for using the path generation capabilities of computers.

MORPHING: This trendy technique is really a sub-set of path animation. In it, key elements within two different images are tracked as inbetweens. This results in a smooth metamorphosis from one image to the other.

ILLUSTRATION STYLES: To put this simply, computer rendering has absolutely, wonderfully blown apart the expressive universe of pre-computer animation. In ways that are extraordinarily easy, an animator working at his or her desktop console can locate, copy, import, alter, scale, colour, filter, and multiply images in ways that previously took entire professions and dedicated tools.

3-D: Right now it is Three-Dimensional rendering (including texture mapping, lighting and camera movement) that seems to have provided the most fertile new ground for animation. But there's much remaining to do in the refinement and integration of 3-D aesthetics and techniques to traditional 2-D animation principals.

MOTION CAPTURE: This is the new domain that fuses theatre and puppetry with what we know as animation. My colleagues at Colossal Pictures in San Francisco are currently active in this area.

DIGITAL COMPOSITING: Remember "blue screen" techniques in motion pictures? Seamless marriage of different image sources can be done today on accessible, affordable computers using off-the-shelf software. Compression, storage and processing speed will lead to more and more digital compositing. MTV's affinity to compositing seems to have already spawned a bunch of aesthetics here.

XYZ NAVIGATION: In computer games and interactive CD-ROMs we're seeing an exponential evolution of rendered worlds that one flies through with liquid ease. The affinity of computers for such creation of virtual settings is now showing up in all forms of animation, including feature films.

SELF-GENERATING IMAGES: I don't know much about artificial intelligence, but I have seen some work that produces compelling visual worlds that computers have generated without much guidance from a human source. I don't think it's too weird to foresee the day when a computer will choose from among a number of image-based programmes and aesthetic principles in constructing, on its own, intellectual properties that address some question of concern that we have assigned to it.

Those are some of the exciting landmarks. Computers give us tools to serve traditional (and hallowed) forms of animation. They also give us tools for new forms, new voices within animation.

So what does it cost you? You ask. Do you need a Ph.D. in cybernetics or what? What are called "low-end" systems (i.e. less expensive) are generally those which can be assembled from "off-the-shelf" components and software for a base of $5,000. Computer families include Macintosh, Omega, IBM and its PC clones. Additional hardware tools include a Drawing Tablet, Scanner, VCR, and Midi Interface. Don't underestimate the time commitment required to learn how to handle the hardware and software tools — even at the "low-end."

"High-end" systems are usually thought of as those costing more than $10,000. There are many manufacturers, most of which have their own proprietary software. An independent animator could easily spend $50,000 to $100,000 to create a hardware base to make their own movies. The more sophisticated and expensive the tools, the more training and computer expertise is required.

The CD-ROM

As mentioned earlier, my most recent venture is the development of a game-based CD-ROM tutorial on animation and its emerging digital forms. *The Animation Tribe* is a model project which combines 3 goals and will produce an experimental, interactive, game-based CD-ROM tutorial. The goals are:

1. To develop a genre of digital publishing that will grab the attention of computer gaming young people (target ages are 11 - 17) and move them toward material of substance in the arts and humanities.

2. To explore the history, aesthetics and creative processes of Animation — one of the most robust 20th century art forms.

3. To challenge interactive and multimedia publishers by setting new standards for the pedagogy of computer based learning.

A longer term goal of the CD-ROM is to create a library of multi-media titles that focus upon those communication forms that touch the lives of young people in our culture. Future computer-based tutorials might be built upon such topics as photography, filmmaking & video, graphic design, drawing & painting, architecture, sculpture, music, dance and more.

Over the past two decades, arts programmes have been jettisoned by school district after school district. More recently, the economic recession has yielded cut-backs in corporate activity in the arts. Governmental support has not been flourishing either. Young people are losing the opportunity to discover what the arts can do — to colour our world, deepen our awareness, give us voice. Humans are symbol makers, first and foremost. We live by gesture, word and image.

Surprising news — last year in the United States, the computer-game industry was larger than the revenues of the movie industry. This brand new marketplace is comprised almost exclusively of young adults and, in particular, by secondary students.

Two questions emerge from this data: What makes computer gaming so compelling? Can interactive software provide what art programmes and institutions cannot? This project will create a prototype CD-ROM that grabs the interest of young people and allows them to mix it up with works of art and with the artists who have created these works. "Grab" is an operational word here. The criteria for our success is simple: our disks must be *so* much fun and *so* satisfying that young people will freely choose to spend hour after hour with them in open competition with all the other media forms vying for their attention. To connect deeply and lastingly, we believe our CD-ROMs must lead users into unfrequented realms of genuine creativity. We must go well beyond what exists within the current definition of "Edutainment," well beyond the computer gaming world of zapping and being zapped.

We must also get beyond the barriers of sexism that exists in computer games. With only the fewest exceptions, the phenomenal growth of computer gaming has resided in space games, dungeons and dragons, arcade games and other forms serving aggressive, competitive needs. Sales demographics show that girls (and probably some boys as well) are left out of the computer world if

they don't like the current kinds of games available.

At its heart, *The Animation Tribe* is about the science of teaching. The central problem of our investigation might be termed the Heuristic of Interactive Media. Everyone knows that computers hold great promise for individualised learning. Everyone knows, too, that entertainment and education are not easily paired. The kind of stand-alone, self-directed learning tool we envision will require a fundamental recasting of existing ideas about "teacher," about "primary materials," about "learner motivation," and about "interface design."

So, why does animation provide such fertile ground for this pilot project? Because it's within the rub of the popular culture that Americans engage most regularly, if not most deeply with the arts. And it is within the indistinct languages of the "pop arts" that the "high arts" are constantly re-energising themselves in the form of fashion, comics, pop music, pulp fiction, posters, movies, magazines, and television. The place to start is within these friendly, accessible forms.

Animation is one of the richest of our popular art forms and it has a fabulous history — from its origins as 19th Century optical toys, through its development within the studio system that yielded the classic character animation of Disney and Hanna-Barbera, to its renaissance during the 1970s and 1980s on MTV as a personal art form, to its present metamorphosis within the realm of digital image making.

Animation is a hot topic with the young people who constitute our target audience. Kids who play computer games already live the rich visual world of animation. Animation is a key interest as well among men in their 30s and 40s — those who constitute the largest group who purchase CD-ROM technology and software.

Another compelling argument for selecting animation as a testing ground for an interactive series about the arts is that, as an art, it incorporates so many other forms including drawing, photography, graphic design, and music. What we learn here will have immediate value in determining what might be next if we go further with a library of interactive titles on the arts.

Our tutorial will incorporate two distinct modes of user interaction. The first might be termed a "tour" through the world of animation: movies, animators, production methods, and artifacts. The interactive strategies we must invest here shall lead to those **critical skills** that are well known in traditional arts education. The second interactive mode represents more of a "plunge" into art making itself. Through a series of "games" that produce original screen-savers, our users will be guided into developing those **creative skills** involved in making animation.

The big challenge is to combine *both* modes of user interaction within one CD-ROM environment. For those who are searching for more information about the world of animation, there will be plenty of examples and explanations which are there when we want them and which are not in our way when we don't. For those who choose to dive into the creative challenges of animation, there will be a range of tools that allow one to explore various animation genres. Hence two kids with very distinct abilities and strengths will find that the experience of the CD-ROM is different for each of them. The "creative" and the "critical" approaches dovetail, of course. Within our CD-ROM's screen environment both these ways of knowing must be constantly bumping into each other, so that one motivates and enforces the other.

We are mindful too that computers are a new medium in their own right. Like all communication forms, the digital media contain inherent qualities that shape and transform the information they carry. Our tutorial about animation must fuse traditional processes and artifacts with an awareness about the new, digital forms of computer technology.

Kit Laybourne is an independent producer/director and author of *The Animation Book* (Crown) and *The Animation Tribe,* an interactive CD-ROM tutorial to be published by The Voyager Company.

Computer Animation Sampler

Computers in support of traditional techniques:

- storyboarding
- ink & paint
- pencil tests
- animatics
- inbetweening
- logos

New aesthetics / techniques born of computer-based technologies:

- path
- morphing
- motion capture
- 3-D
- digital compositing
- XYZ navigation

Low end systems are generally those which can be assembled from "off the shelf" components and software for base of $5,000. Computers include MacIntosh, Omega, IBM / Windows. Additional hardware tools are Drawing Tablet; Scanner; VCR, Sound Cards, Midi interface.

Screening Suggestions

Red Barchetta
Bob Rafei • 21 Overlook Ave, Emerson, N.J.07630 • Hardware (H): MacIntosh Quadra 950; Software (S) Fractal Painter, Photoshop, Mac Tapaz 3-D, Macromind Director

Ruff's Bone
Eli Noyes with Colossal Picture's Multi Media Division for Broderbund • 2800 Third St, San Francisco, CA., 94107 • 415-550-8772 • (H) MacIntosh Quatra 950 & 750; (S) scanned images, Photoshop, Macromind Director

Shadow Puppets
Chuck Gamble • 711 10th Ave East #3, Seattle, WA 98102 • (H) MacIntosh; (S) Macromind Director

Break the Chain
Kyle Baker • 705 Ozone St, Santa Monica, CA., 90405 • (H) MacIntosh Quatra 650; (S) The Animation Stand

Nietzche Pops
Ben Hillman • 27 West 20th St, Suite 1101, NYC 10011 • (H) MacIntosh IIfx; (S) Scanned Drawings, Photoshop, Macromind Director, 3-D vis Electric Image; piece shot in 35mm

Monster Party
Valerie Hallier • 441 East 12th St. #1D, NYC 10019 • (H) MacIntosh for 2D with (S) Adobe Illustrator & Macromind Director; (H) 3-D via SGI platform with (S) TDI's Explorer software

Gas Planet
Eric Darnell & PDI's Character Animation Group • 1111 Karistad Dr, Sunnyvale, CA• contact Monica Corbin - Public Relations / Marketing @ 408-745-6755 • (H) Pacific Data Images proprietary hardware and software output to 35mm

Blockheads
Eli Noyes & Mark Swain for MTV's *Liquid Television* • contact Marie Shell @ NUKO computer graphics enterprise at Colossal Pictures, 101 15th St, San Francisco • 415-252-6620 • (H) SGI Indigo (S) Softimage: Live action taped on Hi-8; motion capture via O.H.P.C. / Biovision 6 camera system

Moxie
George Evelyn & John Stevenson @ UKO / Colossal Pictures for The Cartoon Channel. Contact Brad DeGraf or Marie Shell @ NUKO, 2800 Third Street, San Francisco, CA 94107• 415-550-8772 • Proprietary configurations of hardware and software

Interactive Children's Media

Gary Schwartz

Ten years ago in a small town in Northern Japan, I sat proudly at a pottery wheel eyeing my first success — a tea cup. My Sensei, huddled at a heater in the middle of the room, looked across at my creation, tutted to himself, and began to impress upon me the "art" of cup-making. "Never try to make anything one hundred percent perfectly," he explained. "Always leave a little unfinished so that when the user holds the cup he will have space to share in the making."

The more I experiment in the world of children's media, the more relevant this lesson becomes. Anything that is produced, packaged and sent out to a young, passive audience partially fails. While the product may succeed at the box office or win high ratings on primetime television, it does not allow the end user to "share in the making," and ultimately, the audience is left unempowered and to a large extent ignored.

In this last decade of the century, media is undergoing a revolution as the passive, popcorn-crunching viewer is battling back into the picture. Powerful software platforms such as CD-ROM and CD-I, which play on home computers, are allowing the audience to become part of the production. The young cyber warrior sitting in his or her home or classroom is now scriptwriter, director and cinematographer.

The history of children's media started with the illustrated page. Any parent knows the ritual — the finger jab and punctuated mimicry of the bedtime reading. Starting at toddlerhood, the book is a mini-adventure where the reader uses onomatopoeia and gesturing to invoke subtext beyond the author's wildest imagination. The book is only the starting point to be reinvented at every reading. But books are only flat, two-dimensional documents with defined beginnings and ends. Any adventure must be conjured by the reader outside its covers. In the words of media critic Marshall McLuhan, books in themselves are not a very "plastic medium."

Animation took the illustrated book and brought it to life. The paper-thin characters of the page leaped out of the storybook. Children and adults alike watched transfixed as witches transformed cel by cel into gnarled old hags, smiled as forest creatures pranced in bucolic games and applauded as the hero saved the fair princess.

However, while the characters perform in a three dimensional world, the audience is trapped behind a two dimensional screen. Faced with a captive audience, the animator has the daunting task of "wowing" them to the edge of their seats. The magic of the National Film Board of Canada's shorts and the techno-wizardry of Disney's magic carpet ride, do succeed in pulling the viewer into this imaginary world for a few suspended moments. The talented animator is able to conjure ideas and emotions deep within the audience.

The audience and the film however, are like two ships passing in a dark cinema. By the time the lights are raised and the celluloid strip is sealed away in its tin can, the viewer has long since left. The onus is on the audience, if they are so inclined, to use their ingenuity and imagination to roleplay and conjure up games based on the film. In a classroom context, this would be when the teacher would initiate discussion and debate. A good facilitator will relate the subject back to the children's lives and communities, thus contextualising the film so they can understand how it relates specifically to them. Once this link is established, the debate will ignite, hands will fly and the passive viewer becomes empowered. But this is usually due to the rare ability of good facilitators who, unfortunately, do not come packaged with the film.

Both illustration and animation in this traditional media are preconceived and presented in their finished form to the viewer. To return to the "perfect tea cup" metaphor, traditional type media represents perfect cups, which if made well, get pride of place on the mantel where they'll be viewed time and time again. In contrast, the cup my Sensei wanted to create would continually be transformed in interactive rites such as the tea ceremony, therefore he was describing an essentially plastic medium.

In the new age of interactive media, education is programmed for discovery rather than just instruction, so media which are not plastic can be alienating. This was exemplified in the youth sub-culture of the 1970s, which became involved in video and arcade games. Around the corner from the movie theatre, at the back of the convenience store or lined along the game room, a new medium was in its infancy. The old pinball tables were being replaced by technical gadgetry and children were spending their lunch money huddled at the controls, racing cars and shooting down alien pods on monitors.

Electronic game manufacturers understood children's need to master their environment. Arcade games and later pocket gadgetry put children at the controls, demanding all of their attention and therefore transforming leisure, in this context, to an experience where all faculties are fully engaged. One would never call arcade junkies "viewers" or an "audience." They are fully involved in their task and instead become "users" and "players." The popularity of arcade games was not only a semantical shift, but a monumental change in the way children's learning was perceived. Granted, the arcade was not the optimal educational environment, but indirectly it was the first step in transforming the traditional approach to learning.

The interactive media revolution did not happen overnight, but rather was a case of the technological tail wagging the societal dog. The computer progressively shrunk in size, expanded in power and became increasingly affordable. But it was only when a new software platform arrived with the unlikely name of CD-ROM (Compact Disc - Read Only Memory) that the revolution picked up momentum.

CD-ROM's potential has far exceeded the banalities of its high-tech acronym. It stores a venerable feast of information, including photos, video, text, graphics and audio effects. These effects are instantly available and, most importantly, all of this information can be manipulated by the user from the keyboard controls. This is the *Alice in Wonderland* of technology — one hole has opened into another world that is neither linear nor contiguous. The user, the proverbial Alice, can either plan or presume the next twist in his or her adventure.

Learning institutions, such as museums and science centres, made the first purchases of interactive multimedia stations because they realised the benefits which could be obtained. The heightened participation of the museum goer not only increases the amount of information they retain, it also makes the exhibition process more enjoyable.

The first generation of interactive animation was a step back to the archetypal illustrated book as the software was designed around that linear style. Using computers, developers created interactive story environments that let the child click onto "hotspots" on the screen. Essentially, the only difference between the traditional book and its computer compatriot were click-activated characters, sounds and narrated text.

But few children at the mouse controls were complaining, as this new medium was fun. The problem though, was that since the design did not let the user participate and change the course of action, it could become predictable. Therefore, like a pop-up animated book, it was intriguing once, perhaps twice, but the interactivity could become monotonous. Just like an illustrated book, it had a predetermined beginning and end. Ultimately, the audience did not affect the story in any way.

The first generation of developers were so excited about interactivity that they overlooked its real potential. True, the clicks and beeps did engage the child, but they acted as carrots to invite the child into a learning environment in which the interactivity was not integral to the learning process.

Marshall McLuhan, in his seminal work *Understanding Media*, described two types of media: one that is full of data and leaves little margin for the user to fill, and another that is less succinct and leaves more for the user to interpret. In other words, there is media that demands little participation and another that necessitates completion by its audience. McLuhan's "high participation

model" was essentially pointing towards interactive media. For McLuhan writing thirty years ago, television was the closest example of new media, "TV is, above all, an extension of the sense of touch, which involves a maximal interplay of the senses. The TV child . . . wants involvement, and he cannot accept a fragmentary and merely visualised goal or destiny in learning or in life."

However, interactive media in the 1990s is far closer to this definition. It provides the ideal tools for fully immersing the child in an interactive learning environment. Studies show that students can achieve learning objectives 30 percent faster and perform 25 percent better than students trained by traditional methods. In the home, new media provide a high protein substitute to television's nutritional wasteland.

Unfortunately, the medium does not always steer its content. CD-ROM shelves at retail outlets will, in all likelihood, be mostly stocked with repurposed, low participation material. Hopefully, CD-ROM technology will ultimately champion new and innovative ways of communicating and learning.

The second generation of high-participation interactive media is presently taking the next step in the history of children's media, as now the would-be "CD-ROMer" can become a detective, adventurer, or artist using ingenious tools that allow the child to play in professional editing studios. CD-ROM books have been developed that enable children to create their own protagonist and vicariously adventure through a storyline of their own making, while home movies and photos can provide rich stock footage for children to paint and narrate.

Hopefully, the high-tech world of interactive media will not only be a phenomenon of industrialised nations, but also become part of the educational process in developing countries. Optimists, of whom I am one, see CD-ROM as the great catalyst for the democratisation of technology in the emerging world and anticipate that as hardware costs decrease, the CD-ROM will provide a cheap, accessible platform for audio, video and interactive education all over the world. UNICEF's own involvement and commitment to interactive media signals that this exchange of technology will happen sooner rather than later.

UNICEF, for example, is currently involved in a CD-ROM entitled *My City* in which the user travels through a virtual city making decisions that affect the city's children. Every decision and crisis has an animated consequence, and the players see the effects of their actions. In addition, they can design posters to place about the city, write articles for the city newspaper and start their own personal art shows in the city's gallery. The software is a shell in which the child can adventure, and since there is no preconceived route and no predictable course of events, the tactics and strategy are learned through interaction. For the child, it is an adventure into a world of their own making in which each game is never the same.

The challenge in the coming years will not be improving CD-ROM technology, but rather developing content that fully utilises existing knowledge — content that is relevant and stimulating for children. The only paths to success are to include the child as much as possible in content development, explore new ways to enable the child to control the CD-ROM and make it higher in participation.

Once upon a time there was the storybook. Fifty years later it became animated. In its most recent reincarnation, it has become an interactive CD-ROM disk. In the constantly changing world of media, animation "providers" are likely to find their job description change to animation "facilitators" and CD-based software developers, by necessity or design, must learn the art of pottery. Every new product on the shelf will ideally leave a little unfinished so that the user, clicking at the mouse, will have space to share in the making.

Gary Schwartz is president of the Toronto-based CD-ROM production company I Choose Me, and is currently creating the CD-ROM *My City* in conjunction with UNICEF.

My City

This is a cel-frame animated CD-ROM produced in traditional watercolour and pastel artwork. The goal of the title is to ***empower*** children to understand and act upon issues in their community. We have attempted to make interactively integral to the learning process rather than a device or "dangling carrot" to encourage learning.

My City presents a simulated political reality ; the decisions and stratagem the users use in the software can translate directly into action in their own communities. The issues in this "city" reflect successful and innovative strategies that actual cities have adopted around the world.

The player, as Mayor of a chosen city, must make important civic and social decisions that affect the needs of the city's children. *My City* does not grapple with infrastructural urban concerns such as sewerage and electricity; rather, with the ***moral*** decisions facing a "city-state": areas politicians refer to as soft or discretionary issues. The hard costs of running a city absorb over 70 percent of the budget; the Mayor must creatively use the remainder to address a host of important "human issues".

Captain Planet: Entertainment and Education Do Mix!

Nick Boxer & Dan Gottlieb

Look around you. Our air is filthy. Our increasingly scarce water supply is being contaminated. Forests and other natural habitats are disappearing beneath concrete and asphalt. With every passing day, animal and plant species are extinguished forever, stands of ancient redwoods are cleared and vast expanses of rain forests are reduced to ashes. The greenhouse effect, global warming, destruction of the ozone layer, toxic and radioactive wastes, and overpopulation are just part of the litany of environmental dangers. To adults, the magnitude of the situation seems overwhelming and disheartening.

Fortunately, the word "hopeless" is not part of a child's vocabulary. In 1989, Ted Turner committed the resources of Turner Broadcasting System to create a programme that would entertain children, while at the same time teach them about the increasingly important concept of environmental responsibility. The world's first eco-heroes, *Captain Planet and the Planeteers*, were born!

Captain Planet and the Planeteers, a co-production of TBS Productions and DIC Enterprises, debuted in syndication and on TBS Superstation (cable) in September of 1990. It immediately rose to the top of the ratings charts where it remains today, proving that education doesn't have to come at the expense of entertainment.

After Turner Broadcasting System purchased Hanna-Barbera Cartoons in December 1991, TBS Productions transferred production of *Captain Planet* to Hanna-Barbera, and updated the show's look. Premiering in September 1993, *The New Adventures of Captain Planet*, continued the series' ratings success. Both *Captain Planet and the Planeteers* and *The New Adventures of Captain Planet* air domestically in syndication and on TBS Superstation. Internationally, *Captain Planet* airs in over 60 countries.

The storyline and characters for *Captain Planet* were developed with several goals for the audience in mind. First and foremost, the programme was designed to entertain through dramatic story-telling, compelling characters, and exciting animation, while at the same time educate and inform children about real and relevant environmental and social issues, with the objective of raising their awareness, interest, and involvement in problems which affect their own neighbourhoods and our world as a whole. Secondly, the programme should help to motivate children to seek out more information about environmental and social issues. *Captain Planet* is not intended to be the final word on any subject, but rather to be a jumping-off point for further exploration. The last and possibly most important goal of *Captain Planet* is to empower children and encourage them to become informed and educated decision makers, as well as active members of their local communities.

The Premise of Captain Planet

Gaia, the spirit of the Earth, awakens from a century-long sleep to the pillaging of the planet by a largely oblivious humanity. Fearing for the future, she sends magic rings to five youngsters from around the globe who comprise her team in the battle against further destruction of the Earth. Below is a description of these five "Planeteers:"

- *Kwame* is from Africa and is the conservationist of the group. He has seen forests turn into deserts and wildlife disappear, and does everything in his power to save the world's endangered species.
- *Wheeler* is an impulsive, street-wise teenager from Brooklyn, always ready with a flip remark. He loves to provide comic relief to his fellow Planeteers and to goad the villains.
- *Gi* is from Asia and is a mixture of refined culture and high tech/high style. A student of marine biology, she has a strong scientific understanding of the various ocean ecosystems.

• *Linka,* from Eastern Europe, is the most cerebral of the five Planeteers. She is analytical, with a strong background in computers and music. Hot-tempered and feisty, she is nonetheless a master of logical deduction.

•*Ma-Ti* is from South America and is the youngest of the group. Raised by a Kayapo Indian shaman, he has the hidden knowledge of the rain forest, including the unique healing powers of the great forest's plants.

As these youngsters place Gaia's rings on their fingers, they are magically transported to her home on Hope Island, an uncharted, unpolluted tropical isle far from civilisation. There, Gaia teaches them the secrets of nature. As they learn of their personal power, each identifies with one of the four ancient elements: *earth, fire, water, wind* and a very special new power, *heart,* which symbolises the compassion needed to save the Earth. Through the magic rings, the Planeteers learn to direct their powers in their mission to save the Earth. Finally, they are ready to discover the greatest secret of all.

When the Planeteers join their powers together, beams shoot from their rings, meeting and combining in swirling numbers. Thunder and lighting crash through the sky, and as the Planeteers watch, a new hero literally bursts from the Earth . . . Captain Planet! The environmental superhero, endowed with the powers of the Planeteers rings combined and magnified, demonstrates that the whole is, indeed, greater than the sum of its parts.

Intellectually, Captain Planet has an encyclopedic knowledge of the universe; emotionally, he is a blend of the five disparate personalities and imaginations of the Planeteers. He is a combination of their hearts and souls, and a metaphor for their teamwork and cooperation. If Captain Planet is exposed to toxic wastes, smog, acid rain and other pollutants, his powers are temporarily weakened, and he must return to the Earth to "recharge." Captain Planet has a powerful empathic sense and "feels" the suffering of all fellow creatures — even evil ones. Hence, he does not like to inflict pain, which often requires him to use his wits in addition to his incredible strength to defeat the enemies of Earth. He is also quick-witted and usually has a comic line for the villains.

Although he is an environmental superhero, Captain Planet also realises that he is not the long-term solution to the world's ecological problems. He stresses that people must accept responsibility for the future of Earth. This is exemplified by his recurring line, "The Power is Yours!", a reminder that people, indeed, have the power to bring about change.

Captain Planet only appears in his Captain Planet garb. These are not clothes but elements of the Earth that are integral to his composition. He is able to rearrange his molecular structure to transform himself into the various powers and elements of nature, such as water, wind, fire, ice, etc. His outfit does not represent a specific culture. He has grass-green hair, sky-blue skin, earthy-brown eyes, blood-red chest, gloves and boots, and sunlight-yellow insignia / globe. The globe, on his chest, sometimes flickers and turns gray when he is losing power or is exposed to high levels of pollution.

In each episode, Captain Planet and the Planeteers face a rogues' gallery of larger-than-life eco-villains, including such despicable characters as Verminous Skumm, whose goal is to spread filth and disease, and resource-ravaging ruffians like Duke Nukem and Looten Plunder. Although buffoonish in character, they symbolise real threats to the planet Earth. They pillage natural resources and pollute the water and air. They will stop at nothing to accomplish their evil goals.

The New Adventures of Captain Planet takes kids on heart-stopping adventures - part science, part action, but always rooted in fact. Previous show have dealt with issues as complicated and serious as overpopulation, acid rain, garbage dumps, destruction of forests, smog, nuclear war, global warming, drugs, the cold war, landfills, pesticides, homelessness, and animal testing. Each episode reveals somē aspect of the physical effect of environmental destruction and ends with the same message: that every individual must respect planet Earth and preserve its resources if we are to ensure our survival.

Captain Planet and the Planeteers have provided children all over the world with information to help protect their environment.

And each episode ends with a 30 second epilogue that gives viewers "The Power" to be part of the environmental solution.

"Edu-tainment," Successes and Difficulties

While there has always been children's educational programming and entertainment programming, few shows have successfully merged the two. *Captain Planet* was designed to be both fun *and* informative. The programme has been a success critically and economically, as well as in the ratings. But in breaking new ground, there were a lot of hurdles along the way.

At the onset, finding animation writers who were well-versed enough in environmental issues to build them

seamlessly into an action-adventure plot was extremely difficult. In the early stages of series development, we received premises that were either too literal or that lacked scientific foundation. Working directly with the story editors and the environmental community, series producers struggled to find a proper balance. Even after five years of production, we still strive to find the fine balance that maintains strong story-telling without compromising educational content.

Another issue that had to be dealt with is the fact that excessive violence is common in entertainment programming. Many action-adventure series present heroes who use violence as an acceptable problem solving technique. However, indiscriminate violence used purely for its entertainment value is contradictory to the *Captain Planet* ethic. We do not allow the heroes in our series to punch or kick the villains. Because violence is associated with action and excitement, we have had to work overtime to ensure that our episodes are dramatic and action-packed. At the same time, our heroes strive to resolve conflict rather than to escalate it.

Lastly, the use of villains to delineate good and evil in a storyline is common in action-adventure series. However, given that we deal with real-life issues, we were concerned children might come to the conclusion that if their parents worked in a polluting industry that they were somehow villains. Although our show is basically realistic, our eco-villains are intentionally exaggerated so that they are clearly operating outside of the law. They are symbolic of the environmental problems rather than representative of the actions of individuals. We are careful not to be critical of business/industry, but to encourage responsible business practices and a balance between the needs of people, environment/ wildlife, and industry.

Captain Planet in Action

Captain Planet has become synonymous with caring for the environment. Over the five seasons the show has been on the air, we have collaborated with numerous public and private sector organisations to create environmental awareness. *Captain Planet* has "combined powers" with numerous organisations and individuals. For example, the programme has been recognised by Carole Browner and William Reilly, the last two directors of the United States Environmental Protection Agency (EPA), as providing valuable support to the EPA's efforts. Ms. Browner particularly praised the episode entitled "Jail House Flock," for informing both children and adults about the importance of wetlands. *Captain Planet*'s producers created a public service announcement which was added to the end of the show and provided viewers with the EPA's toll-free number to call and receive more information about wetlands. Other organisations *Captain Planet* has collaborated with include the US Fish and Wildlife Service, the American Public Transit Association and Sebastian International's Little Green Programme.

Captain Planet has also made an effort to encourage the marketplace to adopt more environmentally sensitive business practices. *Captain Planet* licensees are required to use recycled materials whenever possible in packaging, toys, and production processes, reduce packaging ad waste, use biodegradable inks, etc. In addition, no "one-time," disposable products are licensed, and most *Captain Planet* merchandise contains an "eco-tip," informing kids of additional ways they can help to protect the environment.

Captain Planet character Gaia, the Spirit of the Earth, sends magic rings to five youngsters from around the world.

The programme serves as a tool to educate the child on environmental problems by offering ways in which he or she can contribute to the solution. There are three needs for the child that are provided by *Captain Planet*. First, is the *intellectual need*. Each episode reveals the impact and physical effects of environmental destruction. The theme of each episode is summarised in a 30 second tag which instructs children on how they can become more environmentally responsible (i.e. recycling cans, bottles, newspapers, etc.). Secondly, is the *social need*. Through teamwork, Captain Planet and the five Planeteers are able to overcome the eco-villains. This sense of unity demonstrates the power of a cohesive effort and instructs children to involve their families and friends in the global awareness effort by setting an example. Lastly, the programme strives to fulfil an *emotional need*. The cultural diversity presented in the segments promotes the understanding of differences among races and provides an emotional support for the child audience. It emphasises that cooperation, compromise and teamwork are all essential in order to create an international awareness of the Earth's fragile environment.

In an additional effort to empower children to bring about positive environmental change in their own communities, Turner Broadcasting System created the Captain Planet Foundation, a

Captain Planet and the Planeteers face a rogue gallery of larger-than-life eco-villians, whose goal it is to spread disease and filth and ravage the earth.

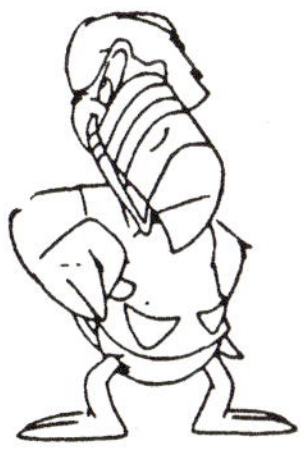

non-profit organisation which gives small monetary grants to children for grassroots environmental projects. The Captain Planet Foundation is funded through a portion of the series' licensing and merchandising revenue.

In conjunction with Turner Educational Series and the Internet system America Online, the Captain Planet Foundation is developing an on-line children's environmental information network. This computer programme will provide a series of turn-key environmental projects for kids — projects like "How to Clean a Lake or Stream," "How to Build a Compositing Centre," or "How to Build a Nature Trail." Local children's groups can apply to the Captain Planet Foundation for funding for both turn-key projects as well as projects they may develop on their own. Other elements of the on-line programme will include conferences with environmental experts, an electronic billboard where kids can leave questions for Captain Planet, and a resource centre where kids can get information about other environmental organisations and publications.

"Edu-tainment Works

Research and feedback has proven that the *Captain Planet* series really works. To date, the series has received three Daytime Emmy Nominations, three Environmental Media Awards, a Parent's Choice Award, two Genesis Awards for animal issues programming, a commendation from Peggy Charren's Action for Children's Television, and numerous other educational and media accolades.

In the United States alone, *Captain Planet* reaches over seven million people a week. In addition, the show airs in over 60 countries, including Australia, most of South America and China. From a distribution standpoint, the series has been extremely successful.

The volume of letters and other feedback *Captain Planet* receives from kids, parents, educators, and environmentalists indicates the series has indeed had a far-reaching impact. Parents tell us that their children are more aware of the environment and its importance as a result of watching *Captain Planet*. They say their kids are more likely to conserve energy, recycle, protect the environment, and encourage others to do the same. Teachers tell us our shows are an excellent classroom tool to initiate discussion about environmental issues, as well as getting kids involved in recycling and community clean-up programmes. The Department of Agriculture, America Public Transit Association, Bat Conservation International, and other groups all use episodes of *Captain Planet* in their in-school programmes. And children love the show too! We receive mail from kids in Ghana, Australia, Singapore, etc. who all want to be Planeteers. Our young viewers are also quick to express the idea that the power is theirs to create a cleaner, greener future.

By all counts, we feel confident that *Captain Planet* provides children with quality entertainment, while at the same time giving them information that will help them become informed and responsible decision-makers for the planet.

Nick Boxer is an award-winning producer of environmental specials and documentaries and is the Executive Producer of *Captain Planet and the Planeteers* and *The New Adventures of Captain Planet* for Turner Broadcasting.

Dan Gottlieb is the Associate Producer of *Captain Planet and the Planeteers* and *The New Adventures of Captain Planet* for Turner Broadcasting.

Street Kids International

Christopher Lowry

Karate is a street educator who tells the story of his own struggle with drugs in *Goldtooth*

They are known by many different names: *malapipe* in South Africa, meaning 'those who sleep in drainpipes,' *changudoa* in Tanzania after the tiny, useless fish which fishermen throw back into the sea, *palomas, gamines*, or *deshables* in various Latin American countries. They are the 100 million girls and boys who live and work in the streets of the world's cities.

Street children and youth in cities all over the world live in conditions of severe stress. They experience serious emotional and physical abuse, and have limited access to education or health care. These assaults on their dignity come from relatives, authority figures, and other youths who have also been born into this violent milieu. It is not surprising that drug abuse is common. They turn to drugs in order to tolerate the intolerable, to rise above pain that no child should have to endure, and simply to deal with the stress of surviving in a hostile adult world where they are marginalised in every way. In one sense, they are using drugs in

A drug dealer confronts Karate and his friends

an effort to improve their mental health.

At Street Kids International, a Toronto-based organisation that works with this population, we believe that unless we are willing to provide these poor boys and girls with homes, warm beds, medical care, schools and protection from abuse, perhaps these children have the right to sniff gasoline or glue and use drugs. Given the same devastating circumstances, many of us would surely do exactly the same thing.

The biggest problem we face as street workers is not the glue or controlled substances used by young people, but the alcohol used by the adults . . . by their parents. We consistently find children who report that their father beats their mother and then beats them because he's drunk all the time. The children flee to the streets. This is an inconsistency which our society tolerates.

Street youth all over the world share a common culture which is characterised by economic marginalisation, the formation of youth gangs in the face of family breakdowns and the misery of slum life, and mistrust of authorities. They value friendship, courage, and ingenuity. They also place primary value on the ability to take care of oneself. This may include the choice to take drugs to feel good and the decision to exchange sex for money, shelter or drugs. Street youth may engage in high-risk behaviour such as unprotected sex or the sharing of needles in order to fulfil their urgent and immediate needs — to improve their well-being. The most effective interventions to promote safe sex and safe drug use among street youth are those that place these actions on the continuum of "taking care of oneself" without actually judging the nature of the sexual activity or drug use.

While young people both in and out of school experiment with a variety of drugs, research indicates that solvent abuse is common among street youth across cultures. The sniffing of glue and other solvents provokes a fast and stupefying high at a very low cost. Solvents, known as "the poor man's high," are easier and cheaper for children to obtain than alcohol or other controlled substances.

Stoned kids are the hardest to reach, and kids suffering from the side effects of substance abuse are extremely difficult to work with. Many educators feel that they're completely unreachable. Substance abuse, including the use of inhalants, is among the most pervasive health issues for street children and youth. It is the most frustrating barrier to effective street outreach. There is a need for effective audiovisual resources available internationally to support substance abuse counselling work with high-risk youth.

Street Kids International subscribes to the Preventive Education model. This notion of preventive education targets the children who are hardest to reach. We may be able to find them, but reaching them and winning their trust is much more difficult. We must overcome formidable defences forged in the streets where these children have lost all respect for authority, all interest in moral lessons and all fear of rules or warnings about 'risk.' Many people who work with these children are very skeptical, even cynical, about ever changing their behaviour. Indeed, they say that if you can change the health risk habits of street children, you can change anyone.

In an attempt to reach street youth and gain their trust, we realised that we would need effective resources that could stand up to repeated use by educators, that would be enjoyed by young people, and that would become regular educational tools for youth workers. One such resource for this population would be audiovisual materials.

Street Kids International's first animated film, *Karate Kids*, attempted to meet these criteria of effectiveness. *Karate Kids* deals with some of the most pervasive and life-threatening street health issues — AIDS and sexual health. Since 1989, it has been dubbed into 25 languages and welcomed by educators in over one hundred countries as a useful means for outreach and discussion.

A key factor to the success of this type of preventive intervention is that it targets pre-adolescents, ages 8 - 14, before their substance abuse habits and risk-taking attitudes are "hard-wired" so to speak. However, the *Karate Kids* cartoon has proven to be useful with a variety of adult audiences as well. In Mexico, it has been shown to mothers of children at risk to provoke discussion about the hazards of street life. In India, it is used to initiate AIDS discussions among conservative and fearful medical personnel. In many countries, it is used to help community groups begin to open up discussions about AIDS issues. A native Canadian doctor told me that after he presented *Karate Kids*, community elders in Northern Canadian villages were able to speak openly about the need to accept people with AIDS and to provide condoms for the prevention of sexually transmitted diseases.

Initially, there was concern over the availability and acceptability of the video format. People often asked us how it was used and how kids would see it. Even more, what urban projects have VCRs? We have found that if the tape is good enough, people will find a way to show it. The video revolution has now reached the four corners of the earth — where there is electricity, there are VCRs. One problem that we have encountered is that many educators haven't yet realised the power of video as a discussion tool. Many adults with even the best intentions can't talk *with* children. They can only talk *to* them. They see video as a temporary replacement for their own one-way teaching style, rather than as an interactive tool to get the kids talking. This is an area where more training is required, and we hope to stimulate more regional training initiatives in the future to help youth workers make betters use of the videos.

Today, millions of street children around the world know the main character and street leader in the video, Karate. They trust him because he shows them how to take care of themselves. The popular impact of *Karate Kids* led to a strong demand in the field for another Karate Kids cartoon that could help street educators deal with other sensitive street health issues.

To initiate the second project, Street Kids International engaged artists and consultants who were involved in the first *Karate Kids* cartoon, including Academy Award-winning writer / director Derek Lamb and animator Kai Pindal. The production team began brainstorming story ideas for the new cartoon in the spring of 1992, working with the initial concept of a cartoon about decision-making. In May 1992, three members of the team visited Honduras to consult with both Latin American and Afro-Caribbean street kids, as well as youth workers in San Pedro Sula, Triunfo de la Cruz and Tegucigalpa. This field trip convinced the team that the new cartoon should focus on substance abuse, and depict decision-making in the context of this pervasive street health issue.

Several months in 1992 were devoted to raising seed money for the project. At the same time, an ongoing literature review was conducted and the team began to consult widely with youth work practitioners and health professionals to clarify the focus of the story. In the winter of 1992-93, Derek Lamb drafted a story and a simple storyboard which was discussed with a number of creative consultants and youth workers in Toronto, Boston, and New York over a period of several months.

This first story was about a boy and girl who become street children and get involved with substance abuse after their mother is arrested in the market for selling her goods without a permit. However, we found that there were a number of unresolved logical problems within the plot, and the director became convinced that it wasn't adequate to meet the demands of the project. Based on this feedback, Derek Lamb wrote a new story in the spring of 1993 which passed through the difficult process of criticism and discussion with fellow filmmakers, youth workers and substance abuse experts. This new story idea evolved into the first edit of *Karate Kids and The Big Fire.* Derek Lamb and Kai Pindal collaborated to create a storyboard of 350 drawings which could be tested with young audiences. The drawings were coloured and transferred to video, and three language versions were produced — American English, International English, and Spanish. None of these test versions had any music, sound effects, or moving pictures.

Throughout the summer of 1993, *Karate Kids and the Big Fire* was tested by community-based partners serving street youth in seven countries, including India, Zambia and Peru. The reviews were mixed. While the majority of youth and educators who saw the test version liked it, there were several fundamental problems with the story and its messages. The most significant problem with the story was its negative portrayal of the drug user, Karate's older brother Billy, as a bad guy who was ultimately killed. This choice placed the heaviest stigma on the character of the substance user, with whom many street kids

identify. As researcher Dr. Andrew Ball pointed out, "... highlighting other, more 'neutral' consequences of use such as impaired judgement, disturbed consciousness (resulting in accidents), depressed mood, headaches, abdominal pains, etc. is less likely to result in the reinforcement of negative stereotypes and resultant discrimination and persecution."

After all of the field test reports came in, the results were absorbed by the creative team. Derek Lamb faced a very daunting prospect. He quickly became convinced that his second attempt to create a story was not good enough to meet the needs of the audience. It was clear that the *Karate Kids and the Big Fire* story would be adequate, but would not be a film that kids would want to see over and over again like *Karate Kids.* For a third time, Derek went back to the drawing board. However, several key ideas had emerged from the testing process, the most important being the realisation that kids were fascinated by the story of Karate's childhood and they wanted to know more about his own experiences of hardship and substance abuse. This makes sense when one considers that a basic method of trust-building in substance abuse counselling is

Karate's sister confronts her enemy, Goldtooth.

Many of the characters in *Karate Kids* and *Goldtooth* are based on real children in cities like Nairobi, Kenya.

for the outreach worker to establish a bond with the client by telling his or her own story. In field testing, the kids were asking for Karate's story, and they identified with the drug user character, Billy. So, Derek Lamb decided to make use of the best elements of *Karate Kids and the Big Fire* to tell the story of Karate's youth.

The new story, *Karate and Goldtooth* was tested in various forms through the fall and winter of 1993-94 in several community-based projects in Canada, the United States, Mexico and Honduras with youth from several cultures. The story stood up extremely well in testing and while the narration and images evolved in response to feedback, both the structure and visual form of the story remained basically sound. Having passed through extensive critical scrutiny, the final story was flexible and resilient in the ongoing process of fine-tuning. It was necessary to increase the planned length of the cartoon from 18 to 27 minutes to accommodate the new story, and the extended pre-testing added several weeks to the production schedule. Fortunately, there was sufficient latitude in the budget to accommodate this imperative. The final cartoon, entitled *Goldtooth,*

Goldtooth attacks Karate when he tries to protect his sister Nina.

took a year for development and a year for production, and was finished in January 1995.

The ability to create an animated story is a unique skill which is not widely understood and is made more complicated by the demands of a social development project agenda. The lengthy story development process involved in creating *Goldtooth* was entirely dependent on the willingness of the writer to expose his work to the reactions of many "critics," to identify useful suggestions about both content and form, and to assimilate these new ideas into a revised story and drawings that will touch children. This elaborate pre-testing feedback-loop process serves as a very effective "reality check" which tests the effectiveness of the resource with its intended audience until the creative team gets it right.

Producers of resources for street youth are not only accountable to the youth and the educators, but also to the donors and institutional "gatekeepers." It has been important in the development of both the *Karate Kids* films to consult widely and include various international institutions in the development process. Several consultants have been selected on the basis that their views are likely to be representative of more conservative agencies, and their approval of the storyboard is an important indicator of distribution potential.

Over-emphasis on the opinions of "gatekeepers" can be misleading, however. For example, one of our donors expressed complete approval for the rough cut of *Karate Kids and the Big Fire* storyboard video. If the creative team had been dependent on donor approval to proceed, the Big Fire story might have been animated despite serious dramatic and conceptual problems. Fortunately, the complimentary donor was only one voice among many, and the artists went back to the drawing board to create the much more compelling and effective story of *Goldtooth.*

Goldtooth is intended to be an effective participatory learning tool for reframing the old question of drugs in a way that helps to motivate youth to make positive decisions and changes in their lives. In the cartoon, glue sniffing is presented as an example of drug abuse that is available on the street, and it is worked into the Karate adventure story in a manner that provides youth workers with a new way to talk about all forms of substance abuse. It is a trigger video to promote trust and dialogue with the educator. The story emphasises the rewards of friendship, self-respect, and life skills in contrast to the powerful but potentially self-destructive comforts of substance abuse.

Just as *Karate Kids* offers an innovative approach to the way that sex education is provided by community-based organisations, *Goldtooth* is intended to enable youth workers to talk about substance abuse with new insight and honesty. It encourages educators to deal with the emotional needs that are so often at the root of adolescent substance abuse rather than using the counselling approach of "blame-the-victim" and "substance-is-evil." The video will stimulate discussion, and the one-page cover / discussion guide will suggest that educators validate adolescents' needs and feelings, understand the real motives behind adolescent substance abuse, and build on the proven ability of youth to look after themselves.

While the cartoon may be broadcast on television in many countries and is sold to those who are able to pay for it, its primary purpose is to be used in youth work by some of the most courageous and poorly-supported educators in the world. It is distributed at no cost to community-based groups that have no money to buy educational tools for their work. For many filmmakers, it is a privilege to produce material which will be translated into many languages and which aims to cross cultural barriers. The makers of *Goldtooth* are motivated by the knowledge that it will be used to help marginalised and disadvantaged young people in the world's cities. There are many drug education videos and books available, and the selection is bewildering. It is hoped that in this crowded field, *Goldtooth* will fill a need for frank, hard-hitting material that triggers lively and productive discussion.

Christopher Lowry, an award-winning film producer and writer, is a co-founder and Director of Communications Projects at Street Kids International in Toronto, Canada.

Maximo

Leon Joosen & José Carlos Cuentas-Zavala

In 1990, UNICEF began its journey into the world of animation by hosting an Animation for Development Workshop in Prague. The Workshop was intended for animation industry leaders to mingle with UNICEF staffers and encourage the development of new communication initiatives within the organisation. Following the Prague Workshop, a number of the big animation companies started looking at ways in which they could work with UNICEF. Walt Disney Feature Animation decided to embark on a project in Ecuador. As a company, we didn't want to simply go down there and make a film — rather, we wanted to train people in the area to create their own films, so they could continue the process once we had left.

Our goal in enhancing animation in Ecuador as a means of development communication was to develop a character capable of transmitting simple bits of practical health information — in the form of short films or spots — to confront the most frequently encountered problems among children, families and the general public in Ecuador.

In 1991, representatives from Walt Disney Feature Animation travelled to Ecuador, where we met with great enthusiasm and a very propitious environment for the development of the project. We discussed the project with UNICEF staff and several local creative artists. In Quito and Guayaquil, animation was being used rudimentarily. The capabilities and the artists were available — they were simply lacking the specific techniques they needed to carry the more sophisticated jobs through to completion. Cinearte, a local animation company with whom UNICEF had been working for the past five years, was identified as the ideal group with whom to embark on this joint venture.

Our first decision was to choose the initial health issue we would tackle. After much debate and discussion, we chose to do a spot on the importance of immunisation.

After deciding on the subject to be done, we set out to define the parameters for the project. We decided to create a character that would be identified with by people all over Latin America and could convey basic health messages to benefit children and the poor in the region. This character could raise awareness by families and communities in poor urban and rural areas on health and nutrition problems and teach simple and important practices that could help prevent these problems.

Over the next several days of this initial trip, Disney Feature Animation executive Max Howard and Leon Joosen led the group

A baby is immunised in the Maximo spot on immunisation.

© UNICEF

in the process of project designing and shaping. By the end of a week's work, we had developed a character to convey these UNICEF messages — Maximo.

Early development of the Maximo project was often challenging, as Ecuador didn't have the facilities to accommodate the sophisticated animation techniques we used at Disney. Nevertheless, the project slowly began to take shape. Local artists were hired and trained in the concepts of animation and colour, and the Cinearte studio was equipped with state-of-the-art equipment, including an animation camera. We had problems finding appropriate materials to work with — they were virtually non-existent in the local Ecuadorian market. To get the project underway, Disney supplied all of the necessary materials: special paper, pencils, crayons, gloves, paints and brushes, acetates and log sheets.

We were able to organise the group at Cinearte and utilise the members' individual talents in the most effective way. We trained five people in the complete animation process and another thirty specifically on colouring work. Others were taught the art of layout and background design. The animation and colouring process for the Maximo immunisation spot was completed in Ecuador, and two members of Cinearte staff were invited to complete the filming of the spot at the Disney studios in Orlando.

After putting in a good deal of hard work and discussion time on character development and concept, UNICEF, Disney and Cinearte decided that the Maximo character would be a toucan. He was developed through a long research process that looked at different animals and characters peculiar to South America. We wanted Maximo to be a friend to children, a character that people all over the region would recognise and identify with. By doing so, we made Maximo the kind of character that is free to pass on any message that needs to be told.

The Maximo character is a storyteller. As such, he does not personally appear within the story. He is a fun-loving creature who looks in from another dimension on the tales he tells. He is a toucan who can pop up anywhere on the screen. These powers are almost magical, giving him the ability to write in the air with his finger or pull signs out from behind his back.

Maximo is bubbly and playful. He speaks with a little chuckle and his smooth voice puts children at ease. When he stands still, he looks confident and poised. He is never cruel and never mean, but instead has a great sense of humour. Maximo tells jokes and has fun with the stories he tells. He can also be very serious when necessary so that his life-saving messages aren't lost. These messages which Maximo conveys are enhanced by a musical background, created especially for each spot. A song that can be easily remembered facilitates communication and reiterates the message.

A major part of Maximo's personality is his voice. Creating an appropriate voice for him involved an exhaustive talent search in Ecuador. We finally selected the voice of actor Jesse Corti, an American who was born and raised in Venezuela. His accent is slightly American which works well because it adds a neutrality to his character. Because his accent cannot be identified as coming from any specific country, Maximo becomes a citizen of everywhere. Maximo's voice also contains a softness and gentleness important in giving his stories a "grandfather" quality. It is very important that Maximo have the same voice no matter which country he is talking about — he must become recognised for the way he speaks as much as for how he looks. This

Maximo the toucan.

© UNICEF

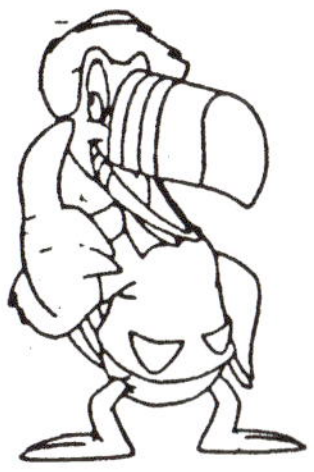

will help children gain trust in him, and will enable him to be recognised on radio spots.

Maximo was first introduced to the Latin and South American region in August 1994 through a national campaign to eradicate measles. The spot, approximately three minutes in length, takes us into a small rural village somewhere in Latin America, where new parents consider immunising their baby. Maximo takes the viewer into the village where we see, through clever animation, the different diseases that could affect their child if they weren't to protect him through vaccination. The story is simple, short and entertaining, and the main points of the message are reiterated by Maximo before he says goodbye.

The immunisation campaign was regarded as successful by health professionals, the mass media and local children and families. In order to promote the campaign successfully, the following promotional products were developed: radio and TV spots, posters, stickers, caps, dolls, press kits, costumes, signs and leaflets. Several other projects were developed as a pilot test for marketing purposes, including mugs, t-shirts, sweatshirts, animation cels, towels and beach bags.

After the measles campaign, summative research was conducted to determine Maximo's impact on the audience. The research showed that Maximo was viewed as credible, he was well-accepted by both children and adults, and that he was perceived as having an international identity rather than solely an Ecuadorian image.

A second Maximo animated spot was created shortly after the initial project, this one dealing with the issue of Iodine Deficiency Disorder (IDD). This spot effectively communicates to mothers that they need a good amount of iodine in their diet to ensure a healthy pregnancy. A number of additional Maximo features have recently been completed in Ecuador on the following subjects: literacy, water and sanitation (sponsored by the Ministry of the Environment), two spots on measles, oral rehydration therapy, and vitamin A deficiency.

It is our hope that Maximo will become a character for all of Latin America, and that each country creates their own stories to be narrated by the toucan. Individual stories from the various countries could be drawn with beautiful local paintings, while others could be created in full animation. Yet others could be done with live-action, or with sand, clay, or puppets.

However, it is terribly important that Maximo remains consistent no matter how varied the stories which he narrates become. The only way to truly achieve consistency is to have all of the Maximo animation created in the same place so that a check can be made to ensure the character does not change. In addition, measures should be taken so that the same voice is used for all the spots.

Though Maximo was conceived with the help of Disney, he needs to be independent and become a character identified solely with UNICEF. Maximo should never be confused as belonging to any other government or non-government organisation. Not only would this give him affiliations that would limit his neutrality and his effectiveness at storytelling, but it would dilute his recognition as a UNICEF character.

As a result of this project, we hope the integration of animation as a new accessible form of development communication is solid within the region. Hopefully, animation will become a part of life and will transmit a feeling of solidarity that will facilitate change in many human attitudes and behaviours benefiting children. Maximo came to life after a two-year process which helped Cinearte in Ecuador to develop a staff skilled in the art of animation and eager to communicate important health messages. The result has been beneficial to both UNICEF and the people of Latin America.

Leon Joosen who has worked on several Walt Disney animated features such as *The Little Mermaid*, worked on the development of Maximo. Most recently, he directed a live-action production on puppet theatre in Burundi for UNICEF.

José Carlos Cuentas-Zavala is the Country Representative for UNICEF Ecuador, and was a key participant in the development of the Maximo project.

African Animation

Bruno Edera

Introduction

This chapter is based on the findings and observations of a research project carried out between April 1992 and April 1993 to compile a database of African animated films. It includes excerpts from the resulting book, *Le Cinéma D'Animation Africain*, which was created as a reference for television stations and other institutions on a generally overlooked area of film animation and to provide background on African films screened at ASIFA's 1993 animation festival in Annecy.

Prior to this compilation, most experienced observers believed the total number of African animated films to be no more than thirty. However, research found the existence of 200 such films, along with a dozen television series representing some 120 episodes of varying length. These numbers indicate that an established animation industry exists in Africa.

In compiling this study, it was vital to be as accurate as possible in focusing on what is meant by the phrase "African animated film." I have used this term in its broadest sense and in a deliberately non-specific way. My definition includes films created by ethnic African artists, produced or co-produced either on the African continent or abroad. I also have included films from the African continent that were not necessarily created by indigenous African artists, but by others born in Africa or those who were residents for several years.

Most people are barely aware that animated films are being made in Africa except perhaps Africans themselves. Even specialists in the field of animation are astonished to learn how many films originate there, and are startled to discover the wide variety of sources behind these productions.

General Considerations

The phenomenon of African animated film should be seen as a dramatically real one, especially now that there is a body of research more comprehensive than anything produced in the past. It is my hope that *Le Cinéma D'Animation Africain* will encourage further studies in this area, as several aspects of our research can be further developed.

It is no secret that various countries in Africa regularly seek technical or cultural assistance from the Western world. In this context, it seems that the animated film, outside of artistic or aesthetic considerations, is an ideal medium for transmitting messages. Animation requires few words—sometimes none at all. Through the visual nature of its messages, the animated medium can tell stories and deliver information while working within traditionally educational frameworks as a force in preserving local culture.

Outside of Africa, many people are already aware of these issues, especially when we consider the impact of television in creating a "global village." Animation can say anything, do anything, and even keep track of the planet's many heroes, whether they come from nearby or from alien worlds. In a number of African countries, we find scattered clusters of individuals who have chosen to communicate through this medium, despite being forced to wrestle with a host of problems that don't exist in countries better endowed in the technology of frame-by-frame expression. Of course, compared with their colleagues in regions where animation is more popular, African artists make up only a microscopic proportion of their countries' populations. We owe these people a vote of thanks for their faith and persistence.

In watching African animation, we find ourselves discovering sometimes within a few minutes another face to this great continent. We become acquainted with different lives, stories and preoccupations than those we see in other means of communication. When conducting my research, I was impressed by the effectiveness of animation as a dynamic means of communication and by the fact that animators have the power to manipulate its strengths, effects and limitations.

Moustapha Alassane from Niger, is one

of the more famous African filmmakers, once told me:

> "... we can pick up TV broadcasts easily in Africa. When it comes to the animated cartoon, what we get mainly is the invasion of the American or Japanese series .... How can we expect our children to see themselves reflected in such programmes? We badly need to provide our children with everything possible to provide them with access to "their" culture. In this area, we have a great responsibility!"

If we look beyond a variety of special problems, we can see that African animated films represent a kaleidoscope of different animation styles. Taken together, they form an art form that should be studied comprehensively in the future.

© Kibushi Ndjate Wooto, Studio Malembe Malembe, 1991
A scene from *Le crapaud chez ses beaux-parents*

Production Infrastructures

When comparing African animated films with forms of animation from other parts of the world, we need to use a relative scale, as production infrastructures are generally not comparable in the fields of technology, equipment, funding, training and distribution. African animation production has only begun in the last quarter of a century, although there are a few earlier pioneers like the Egyptian and Congolese filmmakers whose activity has only recently been brought to light.

Many of today's African filmmakers are either self-taught or have studied in studios outside Africa. Many have contributed to animated films in a variety of countries including the United States, Russia, former Czechoslovakia, Bulgaria, China, Belgium, France, Germany, Great Britain, and Switzerland. Filmmakers trained abroad generally return home with a small list of credits on their resumes, and usually have a final project from their training programme on their sample reel.

We also found filmmakers who learned their craft in Africa, under the tutelage of non-African instructors. Recently, on-site training has become available in film schools and academies that are springing up throughout the continent. For example, the National Cinema Centre and the Advanced Institute for Cinema in Cairo have produced more than twenty films in recent years and the National Film and Television Institute (NAFTI) in Ghana has inspired young filmmakers to make educational films in Burundi and Zaire. There are well-established studios in several African countries — some independent and others affiliated with television stations — but such studios are still the exception.

Evidence from our research indicates that a number of the animated film projects included in *Le Cinéma D'Animation Africain* were co-produced by two or more African partners or in cooperation with companies outside the continent. Most often, television series were co-produced with organisations outside of Africa.

The main reasons for seeking outside co-production support is the simple fact that animation is expensive. Generally, co-production assistance is most often found in the form of technical cooperation, especially in the production of educational films. However, if we look at the creative work of an independent artist or a television series, we often find projects are seeking funding support in addition to technical assistance. The cost of equipment is high for both film and video. In addition, long delays in post-production are common since film laboratories are rare. Many filmmakers end up completing their work outside of Africa.

Some producers do have their own on-site film labs. For example, Niger's Moustapha Alassane, has installed a portable film-developing lab in his studio in Tahou so he can see his film rushes immediately. However, it is worth noting that the lab is feasible only because his water source is so pure that he does not need to filter it. In Niger, as in many other African countries, the air is constantly filled with a fine dust. Because of the electrostatic nature of this dust, it is not possible to create animated drawings on celluloid or animation cels. Therefore, Alassane has been doing his animation with cutout paper or with puppets, or simply by drawing directly on film.

There are a multitude of different animation techniques being utilised in

Africa today. For example, Mauritian filmmaker Veerasamy Parianen uses modelling clay with great skill. In South Africa, where there are several commercial production studios, animator William Kentridge makes outstanding moral and political films by simply drawing with charcoal on a special surface. More traditional animation techniques can be seen in the cartoons of Algeria, Tunisia, and Egypt, where educational television series for children mix live action and animation. An Algerian film created with the aid of a modern computerised paintbox system shows that if you dispense with the need for actual film, you can have immediate results. In Africa, we find that animators are using every conceivable method or mode of animated communication to express themselves.

Safeguarding the African Tradition

The animated film in Africa is now coming into its own in a number of countries. It is being used for advertising or educational purposes in many countries. But animation is also a valuable medium for telling stories, and concerned craftspeople and artists, worried about some of the detrimental aspects of television, have begun to embrace animation as a weapon for cultural battle.

Today, African television offers its young audiences an endless stream of animated series that are worldwide, invasive, and generally out of touch with the culture of the continent. Filmmakers are aware of the huge number of foreign productions that are being shown on their television screens. Many people, especially artists, are determined to protect the authentic heritage of their countries the oral tradition. Animation is one way to accomplish this. There is a large gap between the generations in Africa, and these filmmakers consider it urgent to hold onto these oral stories, not only for themselves, but so that this precious possession can be passed along to future generations. They also hope to show the world outside of their continent just what an African story, fable or legend truly is.

Many African stories feature animals that have an identical nature throughout the continent and are therefore character types ideal for animation. We find toads, frogs, tortoises, sparrow hawks, lizards, and chameleons in most productions by Moustapha Alassane. We also find such characters in a couple of films by Zairean animator Kibushi Ndjate Wooto, such as *The Toad Visits His In-Laws I and II.* These films tell the story of a toad who encounters all kinds of objects and symbolic beings in direct harmony with nature during his travels. Tunisian animator Zouheir Mahjoub has also created an animal adventure in *A Bull in a Honky-Tonk.*

© Mono Abo el Nasar

A scene from *Survival* a film by Egyptian animator and teacher Prof. Mono Abo El Nasar.

Other animated narratives feature typical African characters such as Ananse, a well-known Ghanaian character who appears in at least three unrelated Ghanaian films: *Ananse's Farm*, by John K. Ossei, *Ananse's Story*, by David Ababio, and the pilot for a TV series called *Ananse*, by Kofi Sarpong and Alex Bannerman. In Tunisia, Samir Besbes breathes life into Jah, a mythical character known for his sense of humour and his playful turn of mind with *The Adventures of Jahjhou I and II.*

Conclusion

I feel very strongly that people should pay attention to African animation. It has the potential to eventually attain wide distribution and world-class importance! Such is the hope of many filmmakers and producers. In recent years Africa, especially in areas of culture, music, folklore, theatre and literature, has captured the interest and imagination of a growing number of people around the world. Let us hope that Africa's animated film industry can be used to produce a better understanding of this immense continent and its artistic potential.

Bruno Edera is a specialist in programming and production with a particular focus in animation and short films at Television Suisse Romande in Geneva.

This contribution was translated by
William Mack White

The Somalian Child

Christian Clark

"Children here do not wear shorts," states Aden, my colleague, rather definitively. "And our noses, they are certainly not so big!" It is February 1994. I have just been posted to Mogadiscio, Somalia as an Information Officer with UNICEF. I am with my lanky Somali associate looking at a cartoon I have just drawn for a health leaflet to be distributed throughout this beleaguered Horn of Africa nation. It shows two children by a water pump, one holding up a glass of mucky water. "No, no, no," says the other, refusing to touch the cholera tainted aqua, "I do not drink dirty water!" After some heated discussion with Aden, it is decided the shorts go, but I insist that the noses stay. Pity about the punchline.

Somalia not only has a vibrant yet ancient oral culture, but a relatively recent visual culture as well. The country's orality has, at its roots, a particularly Somali love and appreciation of poetry and a prevalent custom of requiring children, at very early ages, to memorise generations of family and complex clan lineages. The new Somali visual culture, on the other hand, is much more prosaic. It is, by and large, a response to illiteracy rates which are amongst the highest in the world. Indeed, in 1990, the last year statistics for Somalia were available, only 36 percent of men and a paltry 14 percent of women could read and write.

Yet Somalis, an industrious and enterprising people, have found ways around what would be in other countries, crippling rates of illiteracy. As a former cartoonist myself, I was indeed surprised by what I saw on my very first day in this country. For on the dusty exteriors of the squat cement buildings which are the backbone of most Somali commercial districts, are drawn cartoons. Clearly a businessman such as a local butcher in South Mogadiscio, who has vividly painted little blue and gray billy goats frolicking on the outside wall of his establishment, has found out what UNICEF and other aid agencies are only just now learning. In order to capitalise on the particular visual literacy of the Somali people and better "educate" a people who, due to war and continuing insecurity, have little access to education — as well as to play to a quirky Somali appreciation of the cartoon and to humour in general — we need to increase our use of comic "graphics" as a medium of information and communication in our programme activities. In short, cartoons are good business.

It has been said the art of caricature depends on immediately recognisable symbols — a kind of iconography. Indeed, when we study caricature, we in fact study the creation of mythology and the turning of abstract notions into concrete symbols. Although all cartoonists must deal with "hand-me-down" cultural traditions, because completely original types are largely incomprehensible to their audiences, cartoons are by and large universal, and universally appreciated by the "common man." From an institutional context however, cartoons have, until recently, been ignominiously ignored. Usually more commonly associated with the Sunday "funnies" than as a tool to educate children and adults, there are signs that cartoons are belatedly being recognised for the important educational tool that they are.

Today, cartoons are being used by UNICEF Somalia to enhance child survival and development. During the 1994 cholera epidemic in Somalia for example, more than 500,000 anti-cholera cartoon leaflets and some 20,000 posters were distributed country-wide. Two other cartoon projects which have been developed are a publication called *Facts For Life* and an animated short called *The Water Pump*.

Twenty thousand copies of a 74-page Somali version of UNICEF's popular *Facts For Life* has rolled off the press, rewritten, or redrawn at least, as a "graphic novel" by one of Somalia's top cartoonists. This new *Facts For Life* features a day-to-day account of a perplexed Somali mother and father who learn what to do in case of diarrhoea, dysentery, dyptheria and dyslexia.

The idea for the animated short, *The*

© UNICEF

A scene from *TheWater Pump* , by Christian Clark

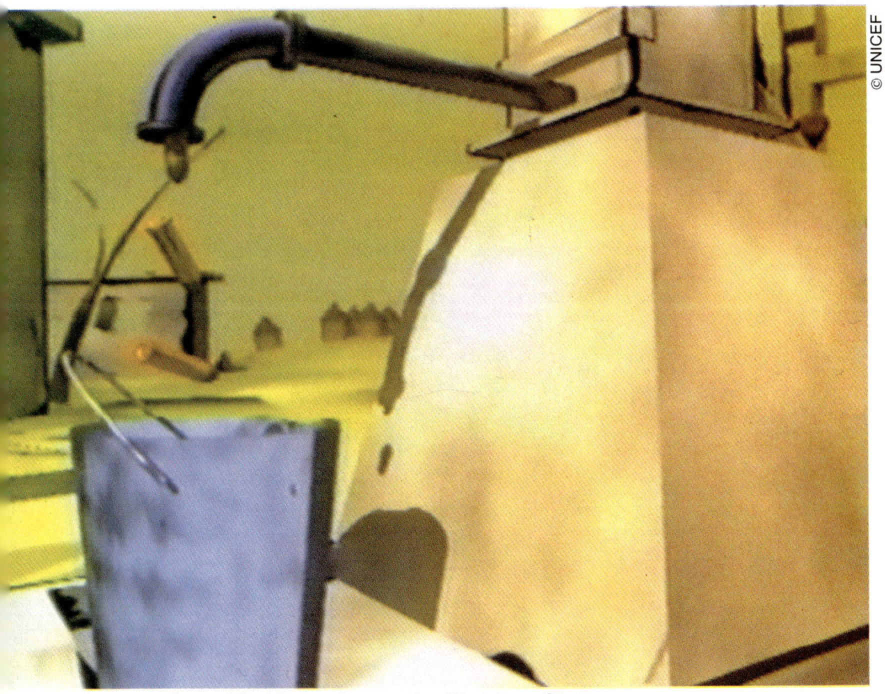

© UNICEF

A scene from *TheWater Pump* , by Christian Clark

water shortage. Indeed, with pastoral nomads making up 80 percent of the population, access to water for cattle and communities could literally mean the difference between life and death. Yet in Somalia, far more money was being spent each year on weapons than on water and sanitation.

With a storyboard in mind for the animated short, the United Nations mission to Somalia (UNOSOM II) was then approached to help underwrite the project. Even though animation has proven to be a popular medium around the world, it is a relatively expensive form of communication. Ultimately, Lansanou Kyote, the Special Representative of the UN Secretary General to Somalia, approved the funding for a joint UNICEF/

Water Pump, came from a weekly cartoon strip started by UNICEF Somalia called *The Kids*. The strip looked at different aspects of life for children living in war zones. One cartoon in particular seemed perfect for animation. It showed two children looking in amazement as bullets fell from the spigot of a water pump rather than the expected water. The cartoon seemed to embody all that was wrong with Somalia, a vast desert country with little arable land and an acute

UNOSOM project — some USD $3,000 in all.

Even if there had been an animation production company in Mogadiscio, Somalia, five years of war had all but destroyed the country's infrastructure. As such, it was decided that Image Ark, an animation production company based in neighbouring Kenya, would do the actual production. Significantly, Image Ark is thought to be the only computer animation

© UNICEF

© UNICEF

© UNICEF

© UNICEF

Above: cartoons from Christian Clark's series *The Kids* on which *The Water Pump* was derived

company south of the Sahara. The three-dimensional, 47-second film took over two months to complete.

The final film *The Water Pump* had its world premiere at the UNICEF animation workshop in Orlando, Florida in November 1994, and has been distributed inside Somalia and worldwide.

By entertaining as they educate, both *Facts For Life* and *The Water Pump* have been shown to be extremely popular in initial audience pre-testing, from Kismayo to Hargeisa, Somalia. Perhaps this is the most graphic indication of the power of the cartoon. If we can get disparate Somali clan members to agree, then we just might be on to something.

Christian Clark, former Information Officer in UNICEF Somalia, is now the Meena Project Coordinator for UNICEF in Kathmandu, Nepal.

Special thanks to

Walt Disney Feature Animation

Academy for Educational Development
Atelier Caméra Enfants Admis
ASIFA
Australian Children's Television Foundation
Bedford Productions, Ltd.
Brasil Press Comunicoes
Cairo Cartoon Studio
Canal 3, Guatemala
Canal 6, Bolivia
Children's Television Workshop
Chocodile Isle
Cineanimadores S.A.
Cinearte
Colossal Pictures
Criaccao
Egypt TV
Fil-Cartoons, Inc.
Filmógrapho
Florida State University
Galler Communications, Inc.
Government of India
Graphoui Workshop
Hanna-Barbera Cartoons
Hiroshima '94 Animation Festival
I Choose Me
International Nutrition Foundation
J. Walter Thompson, Argentina
Jamaican Broadcasting Corporation
John Canemaker Productions, Inc.
Kazkh Red Crescent & Red Cross Society
KV Productions
Lamb Perlman Productions
Mauricio de Sousa Productions
Media Arts
Michael Sporn Animation, Inc.
Ministry of Radio, Film & TV, Beijing
MTV Music Television
Namibian Broadcasting Corporation
National Film Board of Canada
National Film School of Denmark
Nickelodeon
Noyes & Laybourne
On Land Productions
Pakistan Television Corporation
Piramid
Plan International
Producciones Nicobis
Radda Barnen
Ram Mohan Biographics
School of Visual Arts
Shanghai Yilimai Animation Co., Ltd.
Simon Bolivar University
Start Desenhos Animados Ltd.
Street Kids International
Studio Malembe Malembe
Televisa
Television Suisse Romande
Television Trust for the Environment
Today for Tomorrow
Tulane University Medical Center
Turkmenfilm
Turner Broadcasting Systems, Inc.
University of Central Florida
Walt Disney World Co.
Warner Brothers
Winton Hill Animation
World Media Partners
Youth Today

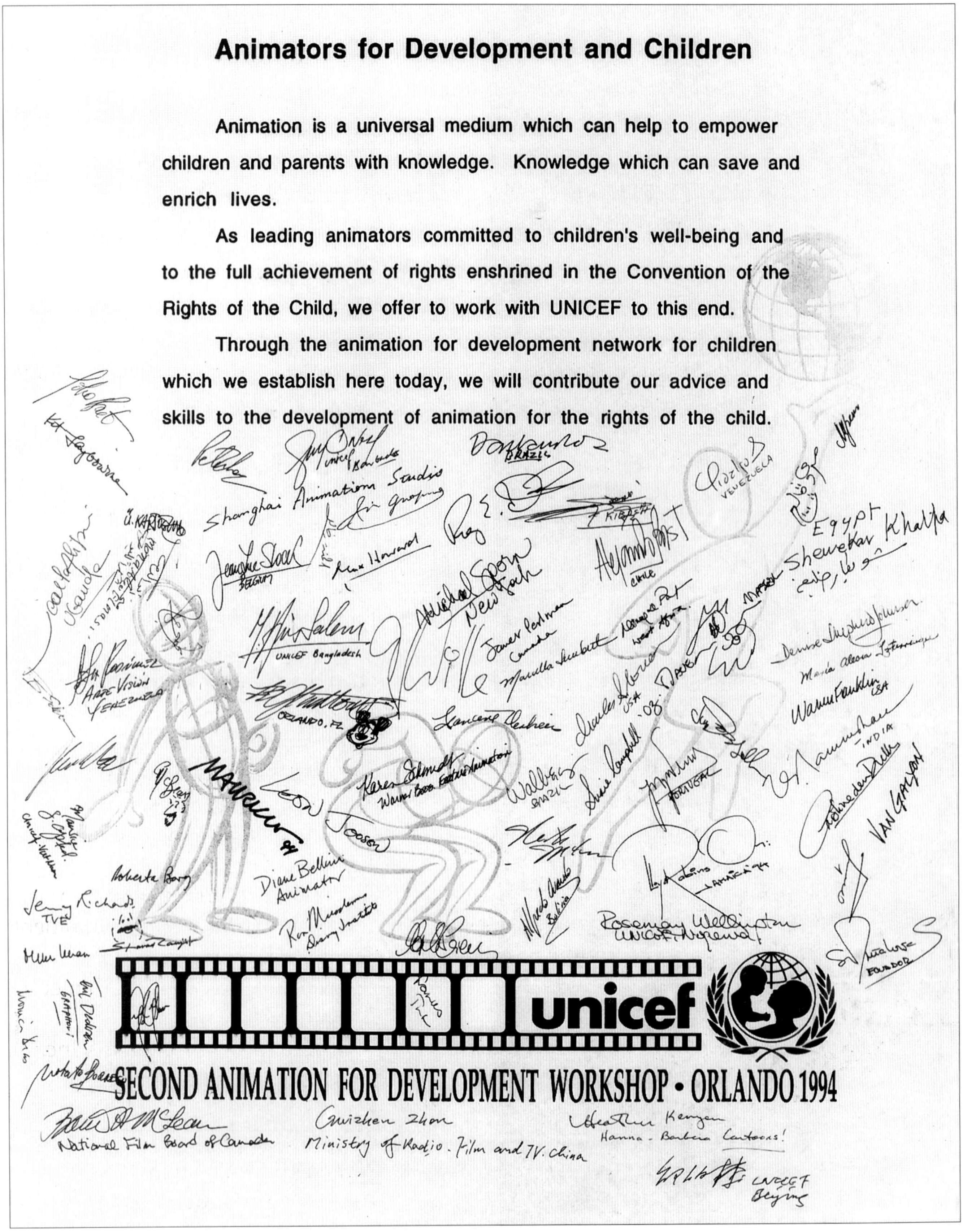

Animators for Development and Children

Animation is a universal medium which can help to empower children and parents with knowledge. Knowledge which can save and enrich lives.

As leading animators committed to children's well-being and to the full achievement of rights enshrined in the Convention of the Rights of the Child, we offer to work with UNICEF to this end.

Through the animation for development network for children which we establish here today, we will contribute our advice and skills to the development of animation for the rights of the child.

unicef

SECOND ANIMATION FOR DEVELOPMENT WORKSHOP • ORLANDO 1994